George H. Tavard

TRINA DEITAS

The Controversy between

Hincmar and Gottschalk

MARQUETTE
UNIVERSITY

PRESS

Marquette Studies in Theology
No. 12

Andrew Tallon, Series Editor

Library of Congress Cataloging-in-Publication Data

Tavard, George H. (George Henry), 1922-
    Trina deitas : the controversy between Hincmar and Gottschalk /
George H. Tavard.
        p.   cm. — (Marquette studues in theology ; #12)
    Includes bibliographical references
    Contents : Foreword — Bibliography — Some relevent dates — The
ninth century — The controversy — Gootschalk's Schedula —
Hincmar's De una: structure — De una: argumentation — De una:
appendices — Lessons of the controversy — Epilogue — Index.
    ISBN 0-87462-636-6
    1. Trinity—History of doctrines—Middle Ages, 600-1500.
2. Hincmar, Archbishop of Reims, ca. 806-882. 3. Gottschalk, 12th
cent. I. Title. II. Series.
BT109.T375 1996
231'.044'09021—dc20   96-35637

Cover photo by Andrew J. Tallon
of Silvacane Abbey Church
Provence, France

Marquette University Press
MILWAUKEE

The Association of Jesuit University Presses

Contents

Foreword

Some years ago I was led, in the context of the Lutheran–Catholic dialogue, to investigate archbishop Hincmar's doctrine of episcopacy (*Episcopacy and Apostolic Succession in the Works of Hincmar of Reims*, in *Theological Studies*, 1973, vol. 34, n. 4, p. 594–623). But it is impossible to read anything by Hincmar of Reims without running into his two polemics with the monk Gottschalk. The better known of these controversies was focused on the theology of predestination, the other on trinitarian language and doctrine. I found at the time that while explanations of the predestinarian controversy are readily available there has been practically no study of the trinitarian controversy. From time to time thereafter I have delved into the relevant writings of both Hincmar and Gottschalk. After poring over the trinitarian texts of the two men I think I have grasped the issues. It is these issues that I wish to explain in the following pages. As this study retrieves a mostly forgotten discussion that took place in the ninth century, it is more strictly historical than my previous publications on the doctrine of the Trinity (*Meditation on the Word*, New York: Paulist Press, 1968; *A Way of Love*, New York: Orbis, 1977; *The Vision of the Trinity*, Washington: University Press of America, 1981; *La Trinité*, Paris: Editions du Cerf, 1992). It should be regarded as a contribution to the history of trinitarian theology, although speculative and constructive theologians may well consider the questions that were then raised as not being entirely obsolete.

Chapter 1 is introductory; with no claim to originality, it analyses the main features of the political and intellectual setting of the ninth century in Carolingian Francia. Chapter 2 explains the origin and traces the main lines of the controversy on the Trinity. Chapter 3 analyzes the relevant writings of Gottschalk. Chapters 4 to 6 analyze the refutation of Gottschalk by Hincmar in his major work, *De una et non trina deitate*. Chapter 7 acts as a conclusion, as it draws some theological lessons for today and tomorrow from what was discussed in the ninth century.

I am deeply indebted to the few who have previously written on Hincmar and on the still fewer who have written on Gottschalk. For

Hincmar, the massive work of Jean Devisse (see below) has been indispensable. But, like most historians who have written about the ninth century, Devisse ventures little into theological discussions.

I have made considerable use of the libraries of Harvard Divinity School, Cambridge, of St. John Seminary, Brighton, of the University of Boston College, Brookline, all of them in Massachusetts, and of the libraries of Marquette University, St. Francis Seminary, and the University of Wisconsin, in Milwaukee, Wisconsin.

Assumption Center
George H. Tavard
Brighton, Massachusetts

Bibliography

Hincmar's surviving writing on the Trinity (*De Una et non trina deitate*) is in Migne, *Patrologia latina* 125. Migne reproduces the text edited by Sirmond in 1645 (2 volumes, Paris: chez Sébastien Cramoisy), which itself reproduces the only known manuscript of this work (Leiden BPL 114, with fragments in Florence, Biblioteca Nazionale, 3.3 1122).

What remains of Hincmar's poems is printed in *Monumenta Germaniae Historica, Poetae Latini Aevi Carolini*, vol.II, Ernst Duemmler, ed., 1884, 409–420.

Ad simplices et rudes suae dioecesis is printed in Wilhelm Grundlach, *Zwei Schriften Hinkmars von Reims* (*Zeitschrift für Kirchengeschichte*, X, 1889, 258–309). The other works of Hincmar provide little or no information on the trinitarian controversy.

Most works of Gottschalk are available in Dom Lambot, *Oeuvres théologiques et grammaticales de Godescalc d'Orbais*, Louvain: *Spicilegium sacrum lovaniense*, 1945.

In addition, Gottschalk's poems are printed in MGH, *Poetae…*, vol.III, *pars prior,* Ludwig Traube, ed., 1886, 724–738.

***

The following titles of secondary literature are intended to assist non-specialists who would look for further reading on the background of the quarrel between Hincmar and Gottschalk. Additional documentation will be cited in footnotes:

Emile Amann, *L'Epoque carolingienne*, Paris: Bloud et Gay, 1947

François Boespflug and Nicolas Lossky, eds., *Nicée II. 787–1987. Douze siècles d'images religieuses*, Paris: Editions du Cerf, 1987.

Maieul Cappuyns, *Jean Scot Erigène*, Bruxelles: Culture et civilisation, 1969

Leo Donald Davis, *The First Seven Ecumenical Councils* (*325–787*). *Their History and Theology*, Wilmington, Delaware: Michael Glazier, 1987

Jean Devisse, *Hincmar et la loi*, Dakar: Université de Dakar, 1962:

Hincmar, archevêque de Reims. 845–882, 3 vol., Geneva: Librairie Droz, 1975–1976

Eleanor Shipley Duckett, *Alcuin, Friend of Charlemagne*, New York: Macmillan, 1951

Francis Dvornik, *The Photian Schism. History and Legend*, Cambridge: Cambridge University Press, 1948

Richard Haugh, *Photius and the Carolingians. The Trinitarian Controversy*, Belmont, MA: Nordland Publishing Company, 1975

Karl Hefele, *The History of the Councils of the Church*, 5 vol., Edinburgh: T. and T. Clark, 1883–1896

Heinrich Fichtenau, *The Carolingian Empire. The Age of Charlemagne*, Oxford: Blackwell, 1957

Hubert Jedin, *Ecumenical Councils of the Catholic Church. An Historical Outline*, Freiburg: Herder and Herder, 1966

Jean Jolivet, *Godescalc d'Orbais et la Trinité. La Méthode de la théologie à l'époque carolingienne*, Paris: Vrin, 1958

Ferdinand Lot and Louis Halphen, *Le Règne de Charles le Chauve (840-851)*, Paris: Bibliothèque de l'Ecole des Hautes Etudes, 1909

Peter R. McKeon, *Hincmar of Laon and Carolingian Politics*, Urbana, IL: University of Illinois Press, 1978

Karl Morrison, *Tradition and Authority in the Western Church, 300–1140*, Princeton: Princeton University Press, 1964

Janet L. Nelson, tr., *The Annals of St-Bertin*, New York: St Martin's Press, 1991

Heinrich Schrörs, *Hinkmar, Erzbischof von Reims. Sein Leben und seine Schriften*, Freiburg: Herder, 1884; reprinted, Hildesheim: Georg Olms Verlagsbuchhandlung, 1967

Martina Stratmann, *Hinkmar von Reims als Verwalter von Bistum und Kirchenprovinz*, Sigmaringen: Jan Thorbecke Verlag, 1991

Walter Ullmann, *The Growth of Papal Government in the Middle Ages. A Study in the Ideological Relation of Clerical to Lay Power*, London: Methuen, 1955

Luitpold Wallach, *Alcuin and Charlemagne. Studies in Carolingian History and Literature*, Ithaca, NY: Cornell University Press, 1959; *Diplomatic Studies in Latin and Greek Documents of the Carolingian Age*, Ithaca, NY: Cornell University Press, 1977

Abbreviations

CC	*Corpus Christianorum*, Turnholt: Brepols
COD	Joseph Alberigo et al.,*Conciliorum Oecumenicorum Decreta*, Basel: Herder, 1962
CSEL	*Corpus Scriptorum Ecclesiasticorum Latinorum*
Mansi	J. D. Mansi, *Sacrorum conciliorum nova et amplissima collectio*
MGH	*Monumenta Germaniae Historica*
PL	Migne, *Patrologia latina*
PG	Migne, *Patrologia graeca*
SC	*Sources chrétiennes*, Paris: Editions du Cerf
ZK	*Zeitschrift für Kirchengeschichte*

Some Relevant Dates

unknown:	– Birth of Hincmar
	– Birth of Gottschalk, son of duke Berno of Saxony
	– Hincmar is placed as a child in monastery of St Denys
	– Gottschalk is placed as a child in monastery of Fulda
844–45	– Hincmar is ordained a priest
	– Gottschalk moves from Fulda to monastery of Orbais
845	– Hincmar becomes archbishop of Reims
848	– Gottschalk's doctrines are denounced to Raban Maurus, archbishop of Mainz
	– The controversy on predestination begins
849	– Hincmar bans the formula, *Te trina deitas*.
	– The controversy on the Trinity beings
	– Synod of Quierzy: Gottschalk is condemned, confined to the monastery of Hautvillers, in the archdiocese of Reims
853	– Synod of Soissons
855	– Synod of Valence: Quierzy is contradicted
860	– Synod of Tusey: compromise on predestination
869	– Death of Gottschalk at Hautvillers
882	– Death of Hincmar at Epernay

Chapter 1
THE CONTEXT OF THE NINTH CENTURY

Politically the Carolingian age started in the eighth century when the Merovingian dynasty of the Western Franks, some of whose later kings had been better suited for the monastic life than for leading armies, was discarded. The dynasty of the Merovingians descended from Clovis, king of the Franks, who had converted from his ancestral paganism to the Catholic faith in 498. It took its name from a more or less legendary ancestor, Mérovée, believed to have died around 417. But the lands that recognized the sovereignty of the Merovingians were never unified. Neustria roughly corresponded to the central Western France of today, South-West of Paris, Austrasia to the area East of Paris, and extending its borders East of the Rhine.

The later Merovingians were assisted by "mayors of the palace," who functioned as majordomos, as prime ministers with full powers, and as military leaders. Pépin d'Héristal, mayor of the palace of Neustria, had made the function hereditary. And there came a time when the leadership of the mayors seemed more promising to the pope than that of their "do-nothing" kings. In 732 at the battle of Poitiers Charles Martel (715-741), mayor of the palace of Neustria since 714, of Neustria and Austrasia since 730, had stopped the advance of the Arabs who were already half-way through Francia. In 751 his son Pépin the Short (751-768), with the consent of Pope Zachary (741-752), was made king of the Franks, thus bringing the Merovingian dynasty to an end. In 768 Pépin was succeeded by his son Charlemagne, who was crowned emperor as the new century opened, at Christmas 800, by Pope Leo III (795-816).

Theologically, the Carolingian age grew from one particular strand in the tapestry of the last period of the Western fathers. That something new was in the making could be observed in Spain in the fifth and sixth centuries, when the councils of Toledo reviewed and reaffirmed the ecclesiastical traditions that had been inherited from patristic times. Through the fifth and sixth centuries these councils set down principles regarding the Trinity that would be passed on to the Carolingians as the authentic expression of the Catholic faith. Meanwhile, theologians of Southern Gaul in the sixth century began to reinterpret the heritage of St. Augustine in the matter of grace and freedom. The first steps that led to the Carolingian age of theology had thus been taken before council II of Nicaea (782).

The Politics of Empire

The political geography of the period gives the picture an extremely diversified coloring. At the death of Charlemagne, in 814, the empire he had created — *imperium Francorum* — remained united, Louis the Pious (778-840) succeeding him with no special difficulty. Louis was Charlemagne's oldest surviving son, and all his younger brothers became, by vocation or rather by design, monks or clerics.[1] But Louis the Pious's sons were driven by ambition for power as soon as they reached the age of maturity, which the Carolingians identified as the early age of fifteen for men and twelve for women.

Louis had three sons from his first queen Ermengard (c.794-818): Lothar (795-855), Pépin of Aquitaine (c.797-838), and Louis the German (c.806-876). Much younger was the only son of Louis's second queen, Judith (married, 818; died, 843), Charles the Bald (823-877). Presumably because of his young age Charles was respectful of the paternal rule and did not join his brothers in open revolt.

When confronted with his sons' ambitions, Emperor Louis the Pious tried to preserve both peace and unity by sharing authority with them in a limited territory, his own superior authority remaining, in principle, intact in the whole realm. There was a normative precedent for this in the tetrarchy of the later Roman empire, when Emperor Diocletian before his abdication in 305[2] divided power between East and West, with one emperor, or Augustus, in each part, each Augustus being assisted by an associate emperor, or Caesar. There also was the recent example of Charlemagne. In 781 the emperor had made his son Pépin, with the agreement of Pope Adrian I, *rex* of Italy,[3] with the task of protecting the papacy and its lands; in 781 Louis the Pious himself had been proclaimed king of Aquitaine. In turn Louis made his son Pépin king of Aquitaine in 814, Lothar coemperor in 817 and king of Italy in 822, Louis king of Bavaria in 825. Such a system, however, depended on the sons' good will to be fully effective. The empire was threatened several times with disintegration.

In 830 Pépin of Aquitaine was able, for a time, to depose his father Louis the Pious, to arrest his stepmother Judith and confine her to a monastery in Poitiers, and to jail some of the emperor's supporters while others fled. He was soon joined by Lothar. But Louis the Pious was able to reverse the situation through separate negotiations with Lothar.

In 833, while Pope Gregory IV (827-844) was on a visit to Francia, another attempt was made, led, this time, by Lothar in conjunction with his two brothers. Again Judith was seized and dispatched to Italy. With the connivance of Archbishop Ebo of Reims and a few other bishops Louis the Pious was forced to confess his "crimes" and enter the Order of Penitents to atone for them, which automatically disqualified him from bearing arms. His young son Charles was forcibly separated from him. At an assembly[4] of the realm held at Compiègne, the rebellious sons received the official ambassadors of Byzantium who had come to see the emperor. But they soon quarrelled, with the result that Louis and Pépin restored their father to power in 834.

Similar turmoil shook the land again in 838. Louis the German had travelled to Italy to meet with his brother Lothar. As soon as he was informed of this the emperor suspected another plot. A meeting with Louis the Pious brought about a straight order that Louis the German remain in his basic territory, now defined as Bavaria. Louis the Pious then hastened to give power to his youngest son, who had now reached the age of fifteen. At the assembly of Quierzy-sur-Oise in the same year of 838 Charles was granted dominion over part of Western Neustria, from Le Mans to the sea. Pépin, now reconciled with his father, supported this action, but he died suddenly at the end of the year. And while this was happening Louis was again seizing cities that were not part of his section of the realm.

Each of these attempts by the sons to gain or increase power was of course supported by a number of more or less powerful lords, usually owners of huge tracts of land. And the ensuing turmoil never failed to bring a degree of stress to the church, as bishops and abbots, the two kinds of religious persons who were officially recognized high spiritual authority, were called upon to take sides. Far away in Rome, the pope kept inviting everyone to peace. But bishops within the realm were not always as wise or as cautious as the bishop of Rome. The position adopted by Ebo of Reims in 833 had far-ranging consequences that directly affected his successor Hincmar.

When Louis the Pious died in 840 the spirit of rivalry again flared up between his sons. Lothar, supported by his nephew Pépin II who had succeeded Pépin I in Aquitaine, tried to take over the entire realm. Only after he was defeated by the combined armies of Louis and Charles at the battle of Fontenoy, near Auxerre, could the succession be settled: in 843 the three brothers agreed to the treaty of Verdun, dividing the territory. Lothar kept the largely honorific title of emperor and took the center, Lotharingia, which stretched from the Netherlands into Italy. Louis the German had the East side of the Rhine. And Charles the Bald, their half-brother, obtained Western Francia. Their nephew Pépin II remained in Aquitaine.

Besides this internal turmoil the realm of the Franks was increasingly subject to raids by diverse groups of Vikings who, swooping down from the Northland, suddenly descended upon a farm, a city, or a monastery, destroying what they could not carry and slaying most of the people they met. Their sleek ships enabled them to go up the navigable rivers far into the land, so that only the people who were a long distance from water could feel safe. The Vikings easily sailed up the Seine and the Rhine. In addition, the southern coasts lay open to the raids of Saracen pirates who crossed the Mediterranean. In 846 the city of Rome was sacked in one such raid. In 848 it was the turn of Marseille to be looted and in great part destroyed.

Unity and Diversity

Caught in the middle of these innumerable tensions, rivalries, coups, and wars, the ordinary inhabitants of the empire still considered themselves to be one people. In reality they were a variegated mix. In the West and in central Lotharingia the Franks predominated, living side by side and intermarrying with the descendants of other Germanic tribes that had crossed the Rhine in the fifth century and with the older occupants of the land, Gallo-Romans, who were an amalgam of Gaulois or Celts and Roman settlers. There were also in Britany and in some mountainous enclaves where the Romans had hardly penetrated (as in the Ardennes, the Vosges, and parts of the Massif Central) purer brands of the Gaulois people. East of the Rhine the Germans, cousins of the Franks, belonged to various tribes that were in the process of merging into one people. They also coexisted at various points of their border territories with the Avars, descendants of the Huns, with Scandinavians (chiefly Frisians who lived mainly within the empire, and Danes, whose king Horic was, in the 840's, allied to the emperor), and with Slavs (chiefly along the Elba: Wilzes,

Sorbs, Obrodites…). Members of all these alien groups were sporadically involved in revolts or raiding parties.

While the people of Eastern Francia spoke their old Germanic dialects, those who lived West of the Rhine — chiefly Franks, Burgundians, Wisigoths — had largely forgotten their original tongue and adopted various forms of popular Latin, from which the later Romance languages were to derive. In the ninth century the language of the Franks who had settled West of the Rhine three centuries before was no longer identical with that of their cousins beyond the Rhine. The oath of Strasbourg by which, on February 14, 842, Louis the German and Charles the Bald swore to stand together against Lothar, was the first written document that featured the Romance language of the Western Franks, in which forms and words derived from Latin were fast replacing Germanic forms and words. This variety of Romance was rapidly gaining ground as the popular lingua franca of Western Francia. Yet the institutions of empire and church preserved the linguistic unity of the whole by keeping standard Latin for most official functions. Though it had evolved in accentuation and in the rhythm of its sentences, their Latin was still identifiable, in grammar and vocabulary, with the classical Latin from which it derived. Charlemagne had been eager to ensure that the Latin liturgy of his realm was of the most authentic form. To that effect he had obtained copies of the Roman ritual, and there took place in Francia a fruitful mixing of Roman texts and Gallic customs in the liturgy. Yet he was not averse to going ahead of Rome when he thought it necessary, and, as we shall see at further length, he endorsed for his realm a modified form of the Nicene Creed that was not in the Roman usage.

Meanwhile there were still poets who composed in Latin with classical scansion. Others pioneered new forms of verse and new cadences. In the early ninth century authors experimented with liturgical hymnody. They created the "sequence," using a form of free verse with no traditional scansion. A monk of St Gall, Notker Balbulus (840-912), a talented composer of sequences, gave the genre an elevated vocabulary with multiple assonances that appealed to the then modern ear. There also were poets who began to compose in the vernacular.

Monasticism

The monastic institution was essential to society and church. It set
the tone for the religious life of everyone. Even though most of the
monks were not ordained, the monasteries were also the main pro-
viders of candidates to the episcopate. They were therefore particularly influential at all levels of church administration and teaching.
Monasteries soon became indispensable in education. The Roman
educational system had broken down in the fifth and sixth centuries
under the impact of the Germanic invasions, though not so much in
the more Romanized southern Gaul (provinces of Narbonne and
Aquitaine) as in the rest of the Gauls. With the growth of the monastic life many foundations were made by Irish monks on the continent in the sixth century. St. Colomban established his first conti-
nental monastery at Annegray in the wooded area of Burgundy that
bordered on Austrasia. The second one, at Luxeuil, was founded in
590. There followed the foundation of St Gall in Switzerland and,
after the destruction of monasteries and the dispersion of monks by
the Lombards, that of Bobbio in Northern Italy, in 614. Some twenty
years later Bobbio adopted the more humane rule of St Benedict.

The example of Bobbio was followed and the rule of St Benedict
became the standard monastic rule in Western Christendom. It was
foreseen throughout the Rule that there would be children in the
monasteries and, at least by implication, that education would be
provided for them.[5] Whence the origin of the monastic schools. Monasteries eventually became the chief centers of learning. Charlemagne
had himself taken the initiative of a revival of learning and therefore
of teaching. In order to extend learning outside of monastic circles
he opened the prestigious Palace School at his court in Aix, that was
to be illustrated by the great name of Alcuin. But he also encouraged
the foundation of cathedral schools established in an episcopal city, a
civitas, that was also often a market center. Under the authority of a
bishop, these institutions were soon to rival the monastic schools.
Out of them the universities would be born in the thirteenth century. They became the main places where boys could get formal education and instruction, the education of girls being left to their family or, for the few who could afford it, to the care of privately hired
tutors.

Parallel to the communities of monks, communities of canons ori-
ented toward pastoral work flourished under Charlemagne. Their

ideal was a union of the active and the contemplative life. Under Charlemagne and his successors some of these canonial communities also became important centers of learning. Alcuin belonged to such a community.

Carolingian Theologians: the First Generation

In the monasteries and the cathedral schools medieval theology began to take shape. The Carolingian period was precisely the time when what is generally called monastic theology emerged. It had been the deliberate policy of Charlemagne to bring the best minds of the times where they could have the most impact, within his empire. Intellectually, the heart of Western Francia was remarkably cosmopolitan. One should not imagine monasteries or episcopal schools as self-centered isolated institutions. The exchange, consultation, and copying of manuscripts required extensive correspondence and travel. Manuscripts were lent and borrowed, often over long distances. Copying centers, such as the one that was created at Reims by Archbishop Hincmar, had to be in touch with the whole Christian world in order to have access to the texts that they were commissioned to copy. Thus Carolingian theology somehow anticipated the later multinational character of universities. But cosmopolitanism does not imply uniformity of thought. It is made of a variety of components. As we shall have occasion to see, in the question of grace and predestination the theology of West Francia North of the Loire river was not identical with that which prevailed south of the Loire.

The most influential of the Carolingian theologians was the Englishman Alcuin (c.735-804), also called Albinus or Flaccius Albuinus. He had been educated at the school of York recently founded by Archbishop Egbert (died, 766) to perpetuate the intellectual tradition of Bede the Venerable (673-735). The school was constituted along canonial lines. Ethelred, or Aelred (died, 781) had succeeded Egbert. Alcuin himself joined the community of canons, became one of the teachers, was ordained a deacon, and directed the school after Ethelred succeeded Egbert as bishop. Being also employed by the king of Northumbria on several missions abroad, Alcuin met Emperor Charlemagne twice. At their second meeting, at Parma in 781 as Alcuin was returning from a mission to Rome on behalf of King Elfwald, Charlemagne persuaded him to move to the imperial court in order to assist in the renovation of education in the empire.

In 782 Alcuin joined the emperor's court at Aix-la-Chapelle, where he taught in the Palace School and became a close friend of the whole imperial family. At some time the emperor put him also in charge of the canonial abbeys of Ferrières and Troyes. In 796, however, he left Aix to head the canonial abbey of St Martin in Tours, where he also directed a school and attracted students from all parts of the empire. Alcuin had considerable influence in the reforms of education and of the liturgy.

Raban Magnentius Maurus (776-856), later called *praeceptor Germaniae*, was by far the most influential churchman in the ninth century. He had himself studied under Alcuin at Tours and he carried this intellectual tradition to the monastery of Fulda in Germany, and hence to the metropolitan see of Mainz. Alcuin's influence also survived into the ninth century through Hilduin (c.770-c.842), abbot of St Denys near Paris, for some years archchaplain at the court of Louis the Pious at Aix, where he was assisted by a younger monk of his abbey, Hincmar, the future archbishop of Reims.

Another religious personality, the Wisigoth Theodulf (c.760-821), had moved from Spain to the imperial court in 781 and was made bishop of Orléans in 786. One may presume that Theodulf was involved in the fight against the remnants of Priscillianism and the adoptianist theories that had gained an audience among bishops, clergy, and laity in his native land. He was a distinguished poet in the classical style and, especially through his authorship of the *Caroline Books*, an influential theological writer.

The Second Generation

This cosmopolitanism was maintained under Charlemagne's successors. The Spanish influence continued. Prudentius of Troyes (died, 866), who took an active part in discussions on predestination, was most probably a Basque whose parents had crossed the Pyrenees at the beginning of Louis the Pious's reign. His name is given in Spanish chronicles as Galindo, and he may have been related to Count Aznar Galindez, who supported Pépin against his father in 833.

Above all, the most impressive philosopher and theologian of the ninth century was Johannes Scotus (John Scot). This Irishman joined the court of Charles the Bald before 847, bringing with him the intellectual tradition of the monasteries of Ireland, where some degree of Greek learning still flourished when it had died everywhere else in

Western Europe. Although he may not have grasped all the nuances of the Greek language and thought, John Scot translated the works of Denys, believed to have been the Areopagite mentioned in the book of Acts (17: 34): *The Celestial Hierarchy, The Ecclesiastical Hierarchy, The Divine Names, The Mystical Theology*, and the *Letters*. This corpus of Dionysian writings soon replaced the translation made by Hilduin, whose Greek was more elementary than that of the Irishman. John Scot's commentaries on *The Celestial Hierarchy, The Ecclesiastical Hierarchy*, and *The Mystical Theology* went one step further. They introduced Platonic philosophy and Greek theology into the West, where, at the hands of the scholastics, the philosophy would have a more brilliant career than the theology.

Abbots were not reluctant to send their young monks away to study under a famous master. This had been the case with Alcuin at Tours. Later, Wettin (active c.824), at the monastery of Reichenau, attracted students from Fulda, Corbie, and other places. Walafried Strabo, Ratramnus, Gottschalk, and possibly Servatus Lupus of Ferrières, studied under him.

The theology of the ninth century, however, never reached the level of serenity that one finds in later monastic works, like those of St Anselm (1033-1109) or of Rupert of Deutz (died, 1133). It was to a large extent a fighting theology, sharpened in the fire of doctrinal disputes.[6] Besides the trinitarian controversy that will retain our attention there were debates on the liturgy, on the eucharist, on predestination. All of them left their mark on later Catholic thinking. At least two of these, on the eucharist and on predestination, were occasioned by the mixed heritage that Augustine had left to Latin Christendom: In what sense was Augustine to be interpreted?

Discussion on Liturgy

Widely diverging explanations of liturgy and ritual were proposed shortly after 820. Amalaire[7] explained liturgy with the help of the allegorical method that was used to draw out the spiritual meanings of Scripture. The movements of the celebrant evoke the journeys of Jesus in Palestine. In the ceremonies that lead to communion, the priest breaks the host in three pieces, thus showing the *corpus triforme* of Christ: the body of his flesh, of the sacrament, and of the church — three in one.

This kind of liturgical exegesis provoked determined opposition on the part of Florus, the most impressive theologian of the primatial city of Lyon.[8] Florus strongly objected to the notion of a *corpus triforme* of Christ. He interpreted it as implying a *corpus tripartitum*, a body in three parts, or even three bodies.[9] Buit he could not tolerate a division of the body of Christ. Such ideas, he thought, were "doctrines of demons." Florus wrote to Drogo of Metz and to other bishops, denouncing Amalaire as a heretic. The synod of Quierzy in 838 agreed with him as it rejected Amalaire's allegorical explanations of the mass as "pseudo-knowledge and novelty of vocabulary."[10] Amalaire was deposed and his predecessor Agobard recalled to Lyon. Yet the question of the *corpus triforme* was not solved thereby.[11] Amalaire had unwittingly opened a cluster of questions.

Controversy on the Eucharist

The discussion of the sacramental presence of Christ started nonpolemically, in the monastery of Corbie, around 831-833. In a book of piety and liturgical theology,[12] Paschasius Radbert (c.790-860, abbot of Corbie in 843, resigned in 849) interpreted the eucharist in an excessively realistic way. The historical body and blood of Christ, now risen, are truly located on the altar once the elements of bread and wine have been liturgically consecrated. They are then received in communion by the faithful.

There was immediate opposition to the work of Paschasius. Raban Maurus, in Mainz, objected to its realism: it is by faith that the communicants become one body with Christ.[13] At the request of Charles the Bald, Ratramnus, a monk at Corbie, presented another view in his *Liber de corpore et sanguine Domini*:[14] the consecrated bread and wine convey the presence of Christ, not physically, but spiritually. There is as much difference between the historical body of Christ and his sacramental body as there is between his historical body and his body which is the church. Yet as he explained holy communion Ratramnus did not focus the presence of Christ on the faith of the communicants but on the symbolic power of the bread and wine that have been consecrated.[15] The two monks did not disagree about Christ being present in the eucharist. Their discussion turned around the symbolic structure of Christian ritual and life and the nature of sacramental symbols.

Two documents relating to this discussion are extant in the manuscript of Gottschalk's works that was discovered by Dom Morin and edited by Dom Lambot. One is a treatise *De corpore et sanguine domini*[16] and the other a much shorter text on the same topic.[17] Gottschalk, who is already, it seems, confined at the abbey of Hautvillers, does not name his adversary. But he attacks the realist interpretation which is that of Paschasius. Gottschalk starts from the faith that "the body and the blood of the Lord are true flesh and true blood."[18] But he is astonished that a text of St Ambrose is claimed to assert that the body born of Mary is eaten in the sacrament. Nowhere, says Gottschalk, has he found such a statement in the works of Ambrose. However, he solves the question with the help of the contested point of view that there are three modes of the body of Christ. Indeed, "one speaks of the body of Christ in three ways: the church, and this mystical body, and that which sits at the right hand of God."[19] The second is the eucharist. The third is the historical body of Christ in its present risen state in heaven. Yet the distinction is not at the level of nature: not *naturaliter sed specialiter*. There is no difference in the nature of the body but only in its *species*, its manifestation:

> ...not indeed naturally, but specially, other is the body of the Lord that is consecrated everyday from the substance of bread and wine for the life of the world through the Holy Spirit, which afterwards is offered with prayer by the priest to God the Father, - and other specially the body of Christ that was born of the Virgin Mary, in which the first is transferred, — and other specially the body of Christ, namely the holy church, and we are this body of Christ when it is given and effected by the action of Christ the high priest (dum ab ipso summo Christo pontifice porrigente tribuitur et confertur)...[20]

Each manifestation is marked by an intervention of the Holy Spirit: at the incarnation, at the consecration, when the Spirit "potentially creates"[21] the flesh of Christ from the bread and his blood from the wine, and of course in the gathering of the faithful in the church. Gottschalk's striking but compact style, however, did not help the clarity of his expression:

> ...we who are the body of Christ eat the body of Christ that is given us by Christ himself from no other than himself for it has been transferred into him, so that to us who are from him that which is in him is

given by him, yet himself remaining unbroken (*integro*), for the body
of Christ born of Mary remains unbroken, in which that which is di-
vinely consecrated to God at the altar is transferred and afterwards
offered and immolated.

Finally, the three modes or forms of the body of Christ do not
divide its unity and identity. There "are not two bodies, far from it
(*quid absit*), but one." This is shown by analogy: Christ is by nature
one spirit in divinity and another spirit in humanity, yet in person
one spirit only; or also the interior man and the exterior man of St
Paul do not make two men, but one only; or man and woman in
matrimony are "one flesh," while remaining two.[22] In other words,
Gottschalk argues that there is a pattern of diversity in unity at several key points of the Christian faith and life. It is this pattern that
explains the unity of the body of Christ and the diversity of its three
modes or *species*.

That Gottschalk's eucharistic theology should have been germane
to that of Ratramnus is hardly surprising. Ratramnus was his friend
and his early supporter in the matter of predestination. Yet I believe
there is more to these texts than a manoeuver by a man who seeks
help in the more difficult situation of the predestinarian controversy.

Controversy on Predestination

This was by far the most important and the most virulent of the
theological polemics of the Carolingian age. The question of predestination was also related to the Augustinian heritage. That it should
take place in the intellectual effervescence of the ninth century is not
entirely surprising. The Carolingian revival of learning entailed an
awakening of the theological mind. Theological acumen gained self-
confidence in the above-mentioned controversies. And there were
questions on the grace of God that were not yet entirely settled. Already in the fifth century the position of the later Augustine on predestination had given rise to doctrinal debates in southern Gaul. Along
with Fulgentius of Ruspe (c.462-527) in North Africa, Prosper of
Aquitaine (5th century) — the probable author of an anti-Pelagian
tractate, *Indiculus de gratia Dei*, to which the name of Pope Celestine
I (422-432) has often been associated — had defended a strict Augustinianism against a former abbot of Lérins, Faustus of Riez (abbot
c.433, bishop of Riez c.458, died c.490).

Faustus was not alone in rejecting the Augustinian view of the consequences of original sin and the human incapacity to choose between good and evil.[23] He stood in the line of Cassian (360-435), whose *Conferences* reflected the monastic traditions of the East, where original sin, its exact nature, and its sequels had never been points of debate. There had also been Vincent of Lérins (died, 450), who saw the Augustinian position as a late accretion to the ancient universal consensus.[24] After several other synods the fifth council of Orange (529), led by St Caesar of Arles (470-543), had endorsed a strict Augustinianism and condemned the positions of Faustus of Riez, that were later given the name of semi-Pelagianism. In so doing, however, the council did not endorse any form of double predestination.

Problems of Church Property

A theological picture of the ninth century would be misleading if one did not mention the extraordinary shape of local churches in the Carolingian empire. For a multitude of reasons dioceses, churches, and monasteries had been heavily endowed in landholdings over several centuries. It had become an accepted practice for bishops to lend lands and buildings to the king or to a lay holder under certain conditions. As it was not unusual for the lay holder to lend it again to someone else, and as such arrangements could last for decades at a time, it was sometimes difficult to know exactly who was the legal owner. Claims and counterclaims of ownership or simply of right to use were often exchanged. And they could easily become a source of ill will and quarrels between ecclesiastical and secular claimants or between bishops and abbots. Part of the confusion came from the not unusual practice of allowing lay landowners to build and provide for private chapels. Along with the chapels private chaplaincies multiplied. Hence more sources of jurisdictional conflicts at local, diocesan, and provincial levels.

In addition, it frequently happened that a diocese owned a church in another diocese with right of appointment to the corresponding benefice, while the local ordinary kept the right to ordain the appointee. This was another potential source of conflicts. Regional and local synods had to adjudicate such matters. Hincmar of Reims was himself involved in that sort of aggravation. He was accused by his nephew, the bishop of Laon, of unlawful appropriation of properties of the diocese of Laon at Aguilcourt. Later he reciprocated by accus-

ing the bishop of Laon of interfering with properties of the diocese
of Reims at Follembray.[25]

False Decretals

This confusion was not without influence on the fabrication of the
False Decretals. This abundant and spurious canonical literature was
composed in a short period of time, in Francia, in a location that has
not been identified. It was not related directly to the main controversies of the period but rather to an underlying malaise in the structure
of ecclesial authority. The main concern of the forgery was to uphold
the rights of bishops as against the authority of chorbishops, of metropolitans, and of provincial councils. By declaring accusations against
bishops to be *majores causae* that could be judged only by the bishop
of Rome, they indirectly enhanced papal power. In the bitter fight
that opposed Hincmar of Reims to his nephew Hincmar of Laon
around 860, the nephew made ample use of them. But the uncle
suspected a forgery when he read supposedly papal and synodal decisions that were absent from all the canonical collections that he knew.
Rothade of Soissons (bishop in 845), who may have introduced them
to Rome when he visited the holy see in 864 to obtain justice at the
hands of the pope, may well have been privy to their origin. Rothade,
who never showed hostility to Ebo of Reims or to Gottschalk, was no
friend of Hincmar.[26]

A Common Thread

It was in the midst of this multifaceted imbroglio that Hincmar
and Gottschalk got involved in their bitter controversy on predestination. Questions about divine grace that had been settled in Roman
Gaul in the sixth century flared up again in the empire of the Franks.
They had been discussed originally in the south, and they reappeared
in the north. While they were debating predestination the two opponents ventured into an additional controversy, on the doctrine of the
Trinity. The first polemic became for Hincmar a hornets' nest. The
two opponents had in fact walked into a trap, the unfinished theology of grace that came from St Augustine. The second remained incon-
clusive. At the horizon of it there was a growing Carolingian tradition on the Trinity. There was also a concern about holy pictures. For
the West was not immune to side-effects of the iconoclastic crisis
that had recently agitated the Eastern Church. But the Franks dis-

trusted Greek theology as much as they envied the wealth of the Byzantine empire.

At this point already one may detect a common thread in the theological debates of the ninth century. The image of the three bodies of Christ, *corpus triforme*, that has its context in liturgy, is evidently related to understanding the eucharist and other sacramental symbols. Liturgical symbols were relevant to the matter of holy pictures. And the question of the nature of Christian symbols was also raised implicitly by the Platonizing thought of John Scot. All these questions turned around representation, spiritual presence, and communication. Furthermore, the battle over predestination was fought between opposite theologies of divine grace. But as both sides - Hincmar like Florus, the council of Quierzy like that of Valence - agreed that grace is God's pure gift, the argument was ultimately about the nature of God's communication with human creatures. It would thus appear that most of the controversies of the ninth century in the empire of the Franks turned around questions of Christian symbolism.

Notes

[1] The emperor's first son, by his concubine Himiltrud, Pépin the Hunchback (c.769-811), had died a monk at the monastery of Prüm, Charlemagne having forced him to retire there in 792 after the failure of one of his several plots against his father's rule. The emperor's sons by later concubines were all sent to monasteries: of the two sons of Regina, Drogo (801-855) became abbot of Luxeuil and then bishop of Metz, and Hugh (c.802-844) abbot of St-Quentin; Theodoric, son of Adalind (807-818), died a young cleric; Richbold (c.800-844), whose mother's name is unknown, became abbot of St-Riquier.

[2] Diocletian had been made emperor in 284.

[3] This was Pépin (777-810), son of Queen Hildegard.

[4] The word, assembly, translates the French "plaid" (Latin *placitum*). This was an "annual or bi-annual gathering of the free men under the Merivingians, reserved to lay and ecclesiastical notables under the Carolingians and the Capetians" (*Trésor de la langue française*, vol. 1, Paris: Gallimard, 1988, p. 463). This ancestor of later parliaments had only a consultative voice; it normally gave advice on the *capitula* or decrees that the king was planning to promulgate.

It often dealt with religious questions. The distinction between such an assembly and a synod or council was never clear, though in principle a synod was a meeting of bishops and abbots called by a metropolitan, though often presided over by the king.

5 Ch. 59 foresees that parents will entrust children to the monastery to be raised as future monks; ch. 63 speaks of "small boys and youths." See Timothy Fry, ed., *The Rule of St. Benedict, in Latin and English with Notes*, Collegeville, MN: Liturgical Press, 1980, p. 270-271; 280-281.

6 One may wonder how many readers a theological author could exoect to have? Before printing made possible the fast multiplication of copies publication could only consist in letting others read and copy what one had written. In these conditions the actual readership of a work was bound to remain small, in spite of work of copyists in monateries and workshops. If the emperor was intrigued by a publication, he could have excerpts made and sent to several theologians who would give their opinion and advice. Perhaps a few dozen only would read a complete theological tractate.

7 Usually called Amalaire (or Amalarius) of Metz, sometimes Amolo or Amolon. He was archbishop of Trèves for a few years (writings in PL 99 and 101), unless the archbishop was a different person with the same name. In any case Amalaire of Metz authored *De ecclesiasticis officiis* around 823 (J. M. Hanssens, ed., *Amalarii episcopi opera liturgica omnia, Studi e Testi* vol. 138-140, Vatican City: Biblioteca Apostolica Vaticana, 1948-1950). He succeeded Agobard of Lyon in 835 when Agobard, archbishop since 833 (writings in PL 104, 9-352), was deposed for his position in the revolt of the sons of Louis the Pious. In Lyon Amalaire's liturgical reforms ran into strong opposition from the deacon Florus, and the new archbishop was deposed by the synod of Quierzy of 838 and Agobard called back. Amalaire retired to Metz, where he died in 852.

8 *De expositione missae* (PL 119, 15-72); the *Opuscula adversus Amalarium* include a letter against the doctrine of *corpus triforme* and Amalaire's liturgical innovations, addressed to bishops Drogo of Metz, Hetti of Trèves, Aldric of Le Mans, Raban Maur of Mainz, and Alberic of Langres (71-80), a speech against Amalaire given at the assembly of Thionville of 835 (94-96), and a much longer address at the synod of Quierzy of September 838 (80-96).

9 PL 119, 83A.

10 PL 119, 84C. Nonetheless some of them were still used in popular missals of the first half of the twentieth century!

11 On the *corpus triforme* see Henri de Lubac, *Corpus Mysticum. L'eucharistie et l'église au moyen âge. Etude historique*, Paris: Aubier, 1949.

12 Beda Paulus, ed., *Pascasius Radbertus, De corpore et sanguine Domini (Corpus christianorum. Continuatio mediaevalis*, XVI), 1969, p.1-131; PL 120, 1267-1350. Paschasius answered his critics in *Epistola ad Fredugardum* (ditto, p.135-173; PL 120, 1354-1366) and in his commentary on the gospel of Matthew, *Expositio in Matheo libri XII*, Beda Paulus, ed., *CC, cont. med.*, LVI-B, p.1288-1299; PL 120, 890-897.

13 *Penitentiale ad Heribaldum* (PL 110, 492-493), in which allusion is made to a previous letter of Raban against Paschasius. This letter is now lost.

14 N. Bakhuizen van den Brink, *Ratramnus. De corpore et sanguine Domini. Texte original et notice bibliographique*, Amsterdam: North Holland Publishing Company, 1974.

15 This debate will influence later controversies on the eucharistic presence, in the eleventh century with Berengar (1000-1088) and in the sixteenth with Zwingli (1484-1531) and Calvin (1509-1564).

16 This document was previously known as *Dicta cujusdam sapientis de corpore et sanguine domini adversus Ratbertum* (PL 112, 1510-1518), and was often attributed to Raban Maur. The style is undoubtedly Gottschalk's. Whether Gottschalk attacked Radbertus before or after Ratramnus did is not known.

17 *Item de corpore et sanguine domini* (Lambot, *Oeuvres*, p.335-337).

18 Lambot, *Oeuvres*, p.324.

19 Lambot, *Oeuvres*, p.326.

20 Lambot, *Oeuvres*, p.327.

21 Lambot, *Oeuvres*, p.325.

22 This is the topic of Gottschalk's second document on the eucharist. In this text Gottschalk adds an unusual and rather strange notion: the mystical (eucharistic) body of Christ is with the divinity of Christ, "which created and consecrated the body and blood of the Lord from the bread and wine," but without his soul, in the absence of which it cannot take the colors of flesh and blood (Lambot, *Oeuvres*, p. 337).

[23] The semi-Pelagianism of Faust of Riez was condemned by a synod of Arles in 473 and a synod of Lyon in 474.

[24] This was the reason for his "rule" about the nature of the Catholic consensus: one should teach only what has been believed "everywhere, always, and by all:" *curandum est ut id teneamus quod ubique, quod semper, quod ab omnibus creditum est* (Adolf Jülicher, ed., *Vincenz von Lerinum. Commonitorium pro catholicae fidei antiquitate et universalitate adversus profanas omnium haereticorum novitates*, 2nd ed., Frankfurt: Verlag Mohr, 1968, p.3). Although Catholic authors have often argued from this rule it can never be applied strictly to any formulation of doctrine.

[25] Peter R. McKeon, *Hincmar*, p.65-84.

[26] On the lingering conflict between Hincmar and Rothade, see Devisse, *Hincmar*, I, p.583-628; Hincmar thought Rothade careless in the administration of his diocese.

Chapter 2
THE CONTROVERSY ON THE TRINITY

The controversies in the course of which the archbishop of Reims and the monk Gottschalk became bitter enemies were started neither by the monk nor by the archbishop. It was Raban Maurus (776-856), the old archbishop of Mainz, who drew the attention of the younger metropolitan of Reims to the doctrinal aberrations of a wandering monk on the question of predestination. The monk, Gottschalk, had just been condemned by a synod of Mainz in October 848. Gottschalk, who had refused to retract, was under arrest. One could question the validity of his condemnation, for he belonged to the abbey of Orbais, in the diocese of Soissons and the ecclesiastical province of Reims, in which he had also been ordained. Raban Maurus therefore took steps to have the monk transferred to Reims under escort, there to be dealt with as the proper authorities, chiefly archbishop Hincmar, would see fit. He also had personal reasons to put distance between himself and Gottschalk.

Gottschalk and Raban Maurus

In the eyes of his contemporaries Raban Maurus was an impressive figure. A prolific though hardly original writer, he acted like the religious conscience of the empire, at least in the Germanic territories, East of the Rhine, in the difficult years of the succession of Louis the Pious.

Offered as a child to the monastery of Fulda, Raban, named Maurus in honor of St Maur, companion of St Benedict, had eventually become a monk. He had been sent to Tours to study under the great Alcuin who, among other things, taught him the principles of poetry. Back in Fulda he had been elected abbot in 822, had resigned in 842 for reasons that may have been related to the political situation, and had been elevated to the episcopate and made archbishop of Mainz in 847. Fulda had been founded in 741 by St Boniface (c.680-754), who had left the British Isles to preach the gospel to the tribes beyond the Rhine and was made missionary bishop for Germany in 722 and archbishop of Mainz in 747. Fulda held the tomb of this apostle of Germany and was the most prominent abbey East of the Rhine.

Raban's opposition to Gottschalk dated from the days when they both lived at the monastery of Fulda. Gottschalk also had been placed at Fulda as a child oblate, and he had also become a monk. He must have been a promising member of the community, for Abbot Egil (died, 822), Raban's predecessor, sent him for studies to the monastery of Reichenau,[1] an island in the lake of Constance. There he studied for two years under a teacher, Wettin (died, late 824), who was famous for his visions. At Fulda or Reichenau Gottschalk befriended Walafrid Strabo, future abbot of Reichenau, who was also a poet, and notably the author of a long poetic narration of Wettin's visions.[2]

It must have been at Reichenau that Gottschalk made the acquaintance of Ratramnus (died after 868), who, as a monk of Corbie, near Amiens, would have a notable theological career, and not only because he opposed Paschasius Radbert (died, 865) on the symbolic nature of the real presence. During the predestinarian controversy Gottschalk sent a poem to Ratramnus, calling him, "friend, lord, father, master."[3] As is explained in these verses, Gottschalk had invited four authors to come out in public and give their view on "the doctrine of the blessed Augustine" which he himself had explained and was defending. So far only three had responded, "Matcaudus, Jonas, and Lupus."[4] When he wrote this, Gottschalk was eagerly waiting for the fourth one, Ratramnus.

Gottschalk, however, had had second thoughts about his monastic vocation and, claiming lack of freedom at the time of his profession, he had petitioned the synod of Mainz of 829 to be released from his vows. The synod so decreed. But Abbot Raban Maurus appealed against the decision to Emperor Louis the Pious. It may have been on this occasion that Raban composed a defense of the practice of placing children in monasteries, and the legitimacy of such a way of vocation.[5] The synod's decision was annulled by the emperor, and Gottschalk was forced to persevere in the monastic life. He was granted, however, a change of venue, and he moved from Fulda to Orbais.

The unlucky Gottschalk, possibly unawares, prepared further difficulties for himself when he was ordained a priest. Some time after 835 he was ordained by a chorbishop of Reims, Rigbold, during a vacancy of the see of Reims. The metropolitan, Ebo, had been deposed in 835 for siding with the sons of Louis the Pious in the revolt of 833. The deposition, decreed at the assembly[6] of Thionville, was of doubtful legality. The archbishop doubted at least the liceity of

Gottschalk's ordination, for the jurisdiction of a chorbishop was unclear, especially in a vacant see.[7] Pope Gregory IV (827-844) was not
involved in the matter.

In any case, Gottschalk left Orbais shortly after his ordination and
journeyed to Italy, presumably with the consent of Bavo, the abbot
of Orbais. He may have made a pilgrimage to Rome. And he spent
some time in Dalmatia and other regions beyond the Alps, preaching
the gospel as an itinerant missionary. He eventually returned to the
Frioul side of the Alps, where he was welcomed by count Eberhard.
He was for a time accompanied by a young man, his nephew.

It was shortly after this that Raban Maurus, now archbishop of
Mainz, heard about Gottschalk's doctrines and decided to intervene.
While he was on a journey with King Louis the German, Raban met
with an Italian monk, Noting, bishop elect of Verona, who acquainted
him with the teachings of Gottschalk about predestination. After
further reflection Raban composed a short tractate *De praedestinatione*,
that he sent to Noting with a covering letter.[8] But Raban now knew
that Gottschalk was in the Frioul territory, and one of his many cor-
respondents was precisely the count of Frioul, Eberhard or, in the
French form of his name, Evrard (died, 867).

Eberhard had considerable political weight, thanks to his wife Gisèle,
daughter of Emperor Louis the Pious, grand-daughter of Charlemagne. This family connection gave him enormous influence. In
addition, the Frioul territory had been created by Charlemagne himself after the conquest of Italy (774). Its geographic location in North-
Eastern Italy made it a key point in the defense of the empire.
Eberhard's royal brothers-in-law, who were often in conflict over power
and territory, carefully cultivated his friendship, and he was instru-
mental in negotiating the treaty of Verdun of 843, which ended the
fight between Lothar and his two brothers. Eberhard was also a pro-
moter of learning. He gathered a library of both religious literature
and secular culture.[9] He was in epistolary relations with several of the
theologians of the times, not least Raban Maurus himself and Abbot
Lupus of Ferrières. Gisèle and Eberhard were the parents of four
daughters and four sons. Both of them had a reputation of piety,
which could not but impress the aging archbishop of Mainz.

Raban sent a long letter to count Eberhard.[10] He did not hide his
hostility to Gottschalk as he summed up the monk's doctrine: "The
rumor has reached these parts that a certain smatterer (*sciolum*),

Gottschalk by name, is staying in your territories (*apud vos*), dogma-
tizing that the predestination of God so constrains everyman that
even if one wants to be saved and strives with right faith and good
works so as to reach eternal life by God's grace, one labors in vain if
one has not been predestined to life…"[11] Raban invited the count to
stop Gottschalk from spreading such dangerous notions.

What Eberhard did is not clear. But Gottschalk made the mistake
of going himself to Mainz to defend his teaching. He appeared before a synod in October 848, in the presence of Louis the German,
defended his theses on predestination, and was condemned for heresy. But the bishops of the province of Mainz had clearly no jurisdiction over a monk of the province of Reims whose alleged heresies had been professed in Italy. For this reason Raban and the synod
of Mainz ordered the monk sent to the proper metropolitan, Hincmar
of Reims.

Hincmar and Gottschalk

The archbishop of Reims was not personally known to Raban
Maurus when, at the end of 848, he received the prisoner and a formal letter sent by Raban in the name of the synod:

> Some gyrovague monk, Gottschalk by name, who claims to have been
> ordained in your jurisdiction (*parochia*), has come to us in Mainz, in-
> troducing new superstitions and a noxious doctrine on the predesti-
> nation of God…saying that the predestination of God is for evil as it is
> for good… We have decreed that, having been condemned along with
> his pernicious doctrine, he be sent to you, so that you may confine him
> in your jurisdiction which he left disorderly… You will please hear
> further from his own mouth what he thinks, and you will correctly
> discern what to do…[12]

At the time, Hincmar was probably not even aware of Gottschalk's
existence. The monk had been gone from Orbais for at least six years,
and Hincmar had been at Reims for only three. At any rate the condemnation was soon confirmed, in the spring of 849, by a synod of
the province of Reims presided by King Charles the Bald, at Quierzy-
sur-Oise.

Another account of the proceedings is given in the *Annals of St
Bertin*:

A man called Gottschalk, a Gaul, a monk and priest of the monastery of Orbais in the diocese of Soissons, puffed up by his learning, had given himself over to certain false teachings. He had got to Italy under the guise of pious motives and had been expelled from there in disgrace. Then he had assailed Dalmatia, Pannonia, and Noricum, constructing with the pestiferous things he said and wrote teachings quite contrary to our salvation, especially on the subject of predestination. At a council of bishops in the presence of Louis, king of the Germans, he was exposed and convicted. After that he was compelled to return to the metropolitan *civitas* of his diocese, namely Reims, where this venerable man Hincmar was in charge. There he was to receive the sentence his perfidy deserved. This most energetic practitioner of the Christian faith, King Charles, summoned a synod of the holy bishops of the Reims archdiocese and ordered Gottschalk to be brought before them. He was duly led forward there, publicly flogged, and compelled to burn the books that contained his teachings.[13]

In having Gottschalk, who refused to recant, whipped in public, the archbishop could argue that he was simply applying chapter 27 of the *Rule of St Benedict* regarding the treatment of obdurate monks. Yet one may wonder if the benevolent measures foreseen by the Rule had been exhausted: The abbot must "adduce care, the unguent of exhortations, the medicines of the Scriptures," and then only may he have recourse to "the ultimate use of excommunication or the plagues of the whip."[14] In addition, Gottschalk was not allowed back to the monastery of Orbais. Henceforth he was confined to the abbey of Hautvillers, in the archdiocese of Reims. He was also, in principle, reduced to perpetual silence. Yet this provision of the sentence of Quierzy remained unapplied. Neither Abbot Halduin of Hautvillers nor, it would seem, the archbishop tried to stop him from studying and writing. Gottschalk promptly proceeded to gather support by inviting several theologians to respond to three questions on predestination. Though only Servatus Lupus's answer has survived,[15] the public debate was launched.

Controversy on Predestination

I would distinguish three interlocking phases in the predestinarian controversy.[16]

The first phase was brief: from the synod of Quierzy, 849, to some time in 850 Raban and Hincmar triumphed over heresy. The synod formulated its doctrine in four chapters (*capitula*). Gottschalk was condemned, and the archbishop composed his first treatise on pre-destination in the form of a pastoral letter, *Ad simplices et rudes suae dioecesis.*[17] Hincmar found strong support in his suffragan Pardule of Laon, who solicited the advice of bishops and theologians, but he had as yet made no special study of the question. Intimations of things to come loomed on the horizon when Hincmar's doctrine was critic-ized in a sermon by the famous deacon, Florus of Lyon,[18] but the archbishop of Reims was generally supported by the incumbent of the most important see of southern Francia, himself Florus's frequent target, Amalaire (died, 852).[19]

The second phase — from 850 to the synod of Quierzy of 853 — was heavily theological. Hincmar was attacked by prominent theo-logians, partly in reaction to a request for further support that he addressed, with documentation, to Amalaire. Ratramnus sided with Gottschalk's strict Augustinian position.[20] Likewise Servatus Lupus, abbot of Ferrières.[21] Prudence of Troyes, while not in entire agree-ment with the monk, severely criticized Hincmar.[22]

Meanwhile, John Scot Eriugena, approached by Hincmar's friend, Pardule of Laon, approved of the condemnation of Gottschalk, but he also contradicted Hincmar and everyone else with an original ver-sion of predestination in the context of his Platonic theology.[23] John Scot's production provoked a huge controversy of its own, Florus of Lyon[24] and Prudence of Troyes[25] composing refutations of his views. Meanwhile, Hincmar made extensive researches in the canonical and theological tradition. In so doing, however, he was misled by the attribution to St Jerome of a Pelagian writing, *De obduratione cordis pharaonis*, and to St Augustine of another one, *Hypomnesticon.*[26] Al-though some of his adversaries pointed out the mistake, Hincmar never changed his mind about the authorship of these treatises. Had he done so his argument from tradition would have been consider-ably weakened. But, relying as he did on these spurious texts, he could not avoid misreading the tradition and the doctrine of Augustine.

The third phase was chiefly conciliar. It went from the synods of Quierzy and of Soissons (called, synod of the five provinces[27]) in 853, to that of Tusey[28] (also called second synod of Toul) in 860, where bishops came from fourteen provinces.[29] The new archbishop of Lyon, Remi (852-875), rallied the bishops of the South and center of France in support of the anti-Pelagian tradition of Southern Gaul (in keeping with the fifth council of Orange, 529). Another violent critique of Hincmar's doctrine and behavior appeared in Lyon.[30] The deacon Florus, who was still acting as the quasi-official theologian of the see of Lyon and who now had the support of Remi, must have contributed to it. But Hincmar ascribed it to Ebo of Grenoble, a nephew of his deposed predecessor Ebo of Reims. Hincmar also blamed Ebo of Grenoble for a sharp attack on himself.[31]

At any rate the synod of Valence of January 855, presided by Emperor Lothar, gathered together fourteen bishops from the provinces of Lyon, Arles, and Vienne. Led by Remi of Lyon, the synod contradicted the *capitula* of Quierzy. In early 859 the southern bishops met at Langres in preparation for Savonnières. They toned down the formulas of Valence. At Savonnières (first synod of Toul) in June 859 opponents and supporters of Hincmar deferred a decision. An agreement was finally reached by the two parties at Tusey in October 860.[32]

Before the agreement of 860 Hincmar issued his second and third treatises on predestination. The second, which also examined several other questions, has been lost. The third defended the *capitula* of Quierzy against those of Valence, drawing on Hincmar's extensive research in the theological and canonical tradition.[33] At Tusey, however, Hincmar consented to make peace with the southerners on the basis of a compromise: The synod agreed on predestination to good, and kept silence on predestination to evil.[34]

The Controversy on the Trinity

It was in the first phase of the polemic on predestination that Hincmar and Gottschalk engaged in their other quarrel, regarding trinitarian vocabulary and doctrine. This happened after the synod of Quierzy of the spring of 849, since Hincmar's accusations against Gottschalk at this synod did not extend to trinitarian doctrine. Only at the synod of Soissons of 853 did Hincmar place Gottschalk's teaching on the Trinity on the agenda, along with the question of predestination and some canonical problems relating to the deposition of Ebo of Reims. The controversy was also posterior to Hincmar's pastoral letter, *Ad simplices et rudes suae dioeceseos.* This letter, written at an uncertain date in 849, warned clergy and people against Gottschalk's teaching on predestination and its consequences for the Christian life, and also, though the point is not explained, against Gottschalk's "presumption" regarding the nature of the vision of God in heaven.[35] But there is not a word about trinitarian theology. This omission would be unthinkable if the controversy had already started In any case, the trinitarian controversy was posterior to Gottschalk's *confessio prolixior*, written in 850, since the question of the Trinity is not mentioned in this statement.

Yet Hincmar's attention must have been brought to trinitarian theology before May 850. In that month Raban Maurus responded to several queries he had received from Hincmar, one of which referred to the Trinity: "Concerning what you said, that there are those who dogmatize that one must believe and profess a trine and one deity, I do not know where they take it from."[36] Clearly, Hincmar had asked the archbishop of Mainz for information and advice. And since Gottschalk's name does not appear in the archbishop's letter it is probable that he was not yet mixed up in the affair.

The point of departure of the trinitarian polemic must therefore be placed in early 850.[37] Hincmar describes as follows the occasion and origin of his interest in the matter:

> It has been a long time since, prompted by the ending of an anonymous hymn which says, *Te trina deitas unaque poscimus*,[38] some persons who take delight in being known for the novelty of their vocabulary, began to contend that one should and may catholicly speak of a trine and one deity, just as of a trine and one God, whence they scribbled their own melody.
>
> Among them, Ratramnus, a monk of Corbie, compiled a sizable book with excerpts from saints Hilary and Augustine, that he addressed to Hildegard, bishop of Meaux. He truncated their sayings and absurdly pulled them toward his own depraved interpretation - just as we read in many Catholic books that it was done at the sixth synod by Macarius, bishop of Antioch.[39] Compared with the authentic texts, this compilation itself denied and refuted its own perverse sense, as anyone who reads will clearly see.
>
> Gottschalk, a pseudomonk of the monastery of Orbais, of the church of Reims, heard it. He heard that I had forbidden to sing in church about a trine deity. Because of his hatred of me, and of his own custom - for since the early days of his vicious youth he has put his delight in trying to find and say new and hitherto unheard of things contrary to the old doctrine of the orthodox, and he has persevered in this attitude - he managed to write a lot and to send [it] to whom he could, first secretly, and then as openly as he could.[40]

This statement is made at the beginning of Hincmar's *De una et non trina deitate*. Composed after the council of Soissons of 853, to which it alludes,[41] this tractate is addressed to "the beloved children of the Catholic Church and to [Hincmar's] coministers," by which I understand the bishops, and specifically those who attended the synod of Soissons. Hincmar had obtained only minimal support against Gottschalk on the problem of *trina deitas*. Only Rudolf of Bourges seems to have responded favorably.[42] The constitution of a file on the matter was Hincmar's attempt to convince the leaders of the church in Francia that a new and dangerous heresy had to be stifled.

Yet there has been some uncertainty about the exact date of Hincmar's tractate. Varying dates have been proposed. It was long held that *De una* must have been written after Gottschalk's death, which took place around 869. However, the conclusion, where Gottschalk's death is mentioned, takes the form of an appendix: *Haec omnia, post librum...*[43] It must have been added by Hincmar after the death of his adversary,[44] when, the polemics being over, he put the final touch to his work. Most of the book was done earlier. Schrörs opted for the year 860.[45] Devisse places it in 855-857. In this case it would have been written some years after the synod of Soissons of 853, at a time when Hincmar wished to justify his harsh treatment of Gottschalk before bishops who felt no hostility toward the monk, and who were more concerned about pastoral problems than about speculation on predestination or on the Trinity. Some five to six years would then have elapsed since the start of the controversy.

These dates, I believe, are too late for the beginning of Hincmar's research on the Trinity, though the last one, 855-857, may well correspond to the termination of the main part of the book. They do not square with the hints given by Hincmar himself. Hincmar provides clear information at the conclusion of *De una* when he describes his attempt to bring Gottschalk to repentance during the monk's last illness, Gottschalk's absolute refusal to recant, and what the archbishop regards as his hopeless death, a point that is made in the chilling conclusion: "He went to his own place" (*abiit in locum suum*[46]). Gottschalk died around 869. But Hincmar began *De una...*, as he declares, "after the book *de praedestinatione*,...as soon as he began to blaspheme about the trine deity."[47]

I take it that "a long time" (*diu*) in the first line of *De una...* refers to the remote origin of the problem, notably to Ratramnus's and

some unnamed others' advocacy of the expression "trine deity."
Unconvinced by these writings, and after receiving Raban Maurus
indecisive answer to his query, Hincmar outlawed the singing of *trina
deitas* in his diocese. It was then, when he heard of the ban, that
Gottschalk made his opinion known.

   As soon as he took cognizance of the monk's challenge of his decision about the trinitarian language of liturgical hymns, Hincmar,
already prejudiced against Gottschalk, initiated a thorough investigation of the question, as he suspected that the monk espoused another major heresy besides the doctrine of double predestination.[48]
Since none of this had happened before the synod of Quierzy of 849,
Hincmar's decision on the hymn must have been made in the late
Spring or the Summer of 849. Gottschalk attacked the archbishop
soon after this, and Hincmar started on his research as soon as he
read Gottschalk's trinitarian pamphlet, the *schedula*. This was in the
Summer of 850 at the latest.

Further Advice from Raban Maurus
   The first mention of the trinitarian question appears in the above
mentioned letter of Raban Maurus. Three letters that were addressed
by Maurus to Hincmar in 850 have been preserved. They were all
written in response to communications that have been lost. The first
dates from March 850. Among other points the archbishop of Mainz
answers a query about new trinitarian teachings. But he knows no
more, and presumably less, than his correspondent. What exactly has
he been asked? One point in Maurus's letter is quite significant:
Maurus mentions Gottschalk and Ratramnus in connection with
predestination. He treats both of them with disdain: "...Gottschalk's
trifles, that Ratramnus's sheet followed" (*nugas Gottschalki quas kartula
Ratramni consequuta est*[49]). In contrast, Raban puts no name on the
query about the Trinity. The ideas in question, which are not described, are simply attributed to some people (*aliquos*).

   Raban was, if possible, more distrustful of Gottschalk than Hincmar
was at the time. Undoubtedly, the connection of the monk's name
with a bizarre or doubtful teaching on the Trinity would have given
Raban an occasion not to be missed to emphasize his horror of the
monk. In his second letter to Hincmar, he did in fact urge the archbishop of Reims to silence Gottschalk for good:

I am surprised at your prudence: you allow this evil man to write, this Gottschalk, who has been found to be blamable in all things, who has shown proper respect neither for his monastic vow nor for the rite of sacred orders and not even for the office of preaching.... Hence it seems good to me, if you agree, that no occasion and permission be given to the said heretic to write and dispute with anyone....[50]

In due time Raban Maurus must have received the acts of Quierzy and the pastoral letter *Ad simplices*. At Quierzy Gottschalk had indeed been absolutely forbidden to communicate with anyone: "We impose perpetual silence on you by the power of the eternal Word" (*perpetuum silentium ori tuo virtute aeterni Verbi imponimus*[51]). This was in keeping with the strict attitude recommended by Raban. Yet Hincmar tolerated the non-enforcement of this part of the sentence.

Neither in his first nor in his second letter does Raban Maurus connect Gottschalk with the trinitarian question that Hincmar has inquired about. Therefore, when Hincmar's first query was sent, late in 849 or early in 850, the archbishop was not yet acquainted with Gottschalk's fondness for *trina deitas*. The second letter does not allude to the Trinity at all.[52] In his third letter, however, Raban returns to the trinitarian problem and admits his incompetence:

Concerning your query whether, according to Gottschalk's teaching, it is licit to speak of the trine and one deity, the trine and one power, and the trine and one wisdom, I wonder what these mean....[53]

One may gather from this that Hincmar has asked Raban Maurus if perchance Gottschalk already spoke of the Trinity, while he was in the archdiocese of Mainz, with what Hincmar regarded as untraditional language. In other words, Hincmar was fishing around, trying to find out if Gottschalk could be saddled with another heresy. This implies that shortly before March 850 the archbishop was acquainted with the monk's use of the formula, *trina deitas*, but he was not yet informed of Gottschalk's argumentation in defense of it. Had he been, there would have been no need to try to obtain further information from Mainz. In any case Maurus does not seem to have taken the trinitarian question to heart, as he had done with predestination.

I see no reason to doubt Hincmar's chronology of the facts. His attention was drawn to theological writings that argued from the language of hymnody in favor of what struck him as untraditional vocabulary and doctrine. The hymn, *Sanctorum meritis inclyta gaudia*, with the verse *Te trina deitas unaque poscimus*, figured in the argumentation. This hymn had originally been spread through the use of a Gothic hymnal,[54] and it was sung in Gaul at vespers of the common of many martyrs. The best known of the authors who approved the questionable expression was Ratramnus of Corbie, the adversary of Paschasius Radbertus in eucharistic theology. Unfortunately, Ratramnus's writing on the Trinity has not come down to us. But this lost piece, that Hincmar knew before banning the expression *trina deitas*, may well have been devoid of reasoned arguments; it may have been chiefly a collection of citations that contained, or were compatible with, the problematic formula, since Hincmar accused Ratramnus of falsifying patristic texts and distorting their meaning. In any case Hincmar failed to be convinced that the formula was doctrinally correct.

After he got acquainted with the texts advanced by Ratramnus, Hincmar considered the matter serious enough to ban the expression *trina deitas* from the hymns in use in his diocese: *trina* was replaced by such words as *summa* or *sancta*. It was only after this ban that Gottschalk intervened. He sided with Ratramnus. This was fair enough: Ratramnus was on his side in the matter of predestination. According to Hincmar, Gottschalk wrote *plurima*, "many things," and, more recently a *schedula*, or sheet, that is quoted in its entirely at the beginning of Hincmar's *De una*.

Several Writings on the Trinity

One may well wonder at this point what were the "many" writings — or perhaps, more simply, the many arguments — of Gottschalk that preceded the *schedula*. One naturally thinks of the documents that were published by Lambot in 1945 from a manuscript that had been discovered by Morin at the municipal library of Bern, Switzerland.[55] Besides several opuscula relating to predestination and to grammar, and some shorter documents on redemption, the soul, the eucharist, the Sybil and other pagan prophets, the manuscript contains four relatively short texts *De trina deitate*, a fifth one that is longer (called *De trinitate* by Lambot), plus a collection of excerpts *De trinitate*, that include passages from Fulgentius, Isidore, Alcuin, and Augustine. In addition, a series of twenty *Responsa de diversis*,[56] addressed to "a critic," begins with five questions of trinitarian theology.[57]

None of these documents can be dated. Given Hincmar's determination to root out Gottschalk's heresies, and the surveillance to which Gottschalk must have been subjected at Hautvillers, one may presume that the archbishop knew all the writings of the imprisoned monk as soon as they found their way into the public domain, and possibly before. But which segments of the Bern collection were already in existence in 850? One may also ask, in what order were they composed?

The documents *De trina deitate* are numbered I, II, III, IV by Lambot, the *Excerpta* being V, and the *Responsa* VI.[58] The *De trinitate*, numbered XIX,[59] is addressed to a fellow monk (*frater*,[60] *frater karissime*[61]). Devisse thinks that *De trina deitate* III is known to Hincmar because it seems to be addressed to the archbishop.[62] But III is made of two separate texts destined to two different persons. The second half of it is undoubtedly addressed to Hincmar, who, though not named, is designated in unmistakable Gottschalkian style by the following string of insults:

> O misella potentiola inflata vesica cutis tumida turgida elata pellis
> morticina...[63]
> ("O miserable puny power, inflated bladder, swollen bloated skin,
> proud dead fleece...")

The contrast with the addressee of the first section of III is striking: "my reader and altogether lover of the truth" (*mi lector et veritatis omnino dilector*[64]). Coming from Gottschalk's pen the two formulations cannot possibly designate the same person. Besides, Gottschalk, who considered Hincmar to be a heretic, and responsible for his own condemnation at Quierzy to be flagellated, to burn his own writings, and to be kept in perpetual confinement and silence (though unenforced, or inadequately enforced), would never have called the archbishop of Reims a lover of truth. Each text ends with an emphatic doxology,[65] as is frequent in Gottschalk's style. We will designate them IIIa and IIIb.

That IIIb is a critical piece addressed to the archbishop is certain. The text opens on an appeal to the example of "the blessed apostles Peter and Paul," models who should be imitated by bishops in Hincmar's ecclesiology. This is followed by a demonstration of the duty to resist authority, even that of a father, a count, a king, or an emperor, if these oppose the authority that is superior to them. The

case of the emperor is the most patent since he has no higher authority but God: "If the emperor wants to sin against God and fight
God" (*Si imperator contra Deum vult peccare et ipsi repugnare*), one
must abandon him and obey God: *imperatorem dimitte et domino deo
te tota devotione summitte.*[66] Applying this principle to the present
question, Gottschalk concludes to the duty of contemptuous disob-
edience when "puny powers contrary to God (*potentiolas deo contrar-
ias*) contradict and resist the divine one and trine power." The next
two pages summarize Gottschalk's trinitarian argumentation. And we
finally learn that the contemptible person to whom Gottschalk is writing
has sent him "three heresies" (*tuas tres hereses quas mihi misisti*)[67] along
with the promise to have him treated with "all humanity" if he consents
to them. But this, Gottschalk claims, would be contrary to the doctrine
of St Paul in Col. 1, 12-14. In these verses, we have been "rescued from
the power of darkness." The implicit conclusion is that Gottschalk would
follow his correspondent into darkness if he shared the three heresies.
Now the only person in authority who tried to make Gottschalk abandon his trinitarian conceptions was the archbishop of Reims.

The addressee of IIIa is called *mi lector et veritatis omnino dilector.*[68]
A similar greeting occurs in *De trina deitate* I: "O my reader and
lover of the truth" (*O mi lector veritatisque dilector*[69]), where the same
person is also called, "my reader whom the Lord God piously loves"
(*lector meus quem pie diligit Dominus Deus*[70]). Further below
Gottschalk tells this person, "I exhort you to be now and ever a lover
of this doctrine of St Augustine…" (*Hortor ut valde sis nunc et istinc
amator illius praefatae beati Augustini sententiae…*)[71] *De trina deitate*
I and IIIa may well have been destined to the same person, who was,
judging from the tone, a well-liked disciple of Gottschalk. The person in question must be other than the addressee of XIX: he is a
brother monk with whom Gottschalk has truly fraternal relations.

As to II and IV, they are short pieces without amenities, notes written to clarify and defend one or two theological points. Their tone is
factual and argumentative. II is addressed to one person, who is simply addressed as *tu*. It argues chiefly from language. IV argues from theological authorities: Augustine, Gregory, the hymns, and Scripture.

Although one cannot be entirely certain, I would think that
Gottschalk addresses three different persons in these writings: a brother
monk (XIX), an inquirer who is also a disciple (I, IIIa), and his de-
tested adversary, Hincmar (II, IIIb, IV).

Trinitarian Vocabulary

Between his second and his third letter to the archbishop of Mainz, however, Hincmar discovered more about Gottschalk's trinitarian vocabulary. He then asked Maurus for information on Hincmar's teaching concerning the conjunction of *deitas, potestas, sapientia* with the expression, *trina et una*.

Now the association of these adjectives occurs in practically all of Gottschalk's trinitarian writings. The order, *trina et una* or *una et trina*, is used indifferently. What the words qualify is usually *deitas*, but, with his usual prolixity, the monk adds many terms to *deitas*, providing long chains of divine attributes, all of which deserve, as he believes, the two qualifiers, one and trine. In Gottschalk's theology not only *deitas* and *divinitas* but also all the divine attributes without exception may be called trine and one. It is likely that Hincmar's inquiring letter cited deity, power, and wisdom as just a sample of Gottschalk's repetitive language.

The *Responsa de diversis* stand by themselves as responses to several queries that have all come from one correspondent. These questions, however, or at least some of them, have been suggested by Gottschalk himself, who admits: "All that I have proposed you should seek is not coming back to my memory at this time."[72] At any rate the questions, Gottschalk also remarks, "are sufficiently old and abstruse, most beautiful and obscure, piously and expertly proposed by previous men and teachers, all or nearly all exhaustively explained with the grace of God."[73] Given the references of *Responsa de diversis* to ideas and arguments contained in Gottschalk's *schedula* and to some points raised in the predestinarian controversy, it appears that Gottschalk is now explaining and clarifying sundry items relating to his two polemics with Hincmar.

Response 4 begins with a critical remark of a general character on errors that are due to a wrong use of the argument from *verisimilitudo*, relying excessively on similarities of language between unrelated problems.[74] This, Gottschalk states, has quite often been done by "latecomers, even some most learned and acute men" (*tardiusculis etiam peritissimis quin acutissimis a viris*[75]). One of these latecomers is undoubtedly Hincmar of Reims; and it is this personage whom Gottschalk has in mind when he hopes that his correspondent will "pay attention to, affirm, and spontaneously appreciate what he [Gottschalk] has explained for the love of God and neighbor," and, reversely, that he will "despise, spurn, and always avoid all lie, which is the devil's son…"[76] It would be hard not to read this reference to the devil's son as a jab at Hincmar.

Gottschalk's heated reaction to the ban on the singing of *trina deitas* may be explained in part by the monk's profound resentment of the archbishop for the treatment that was meted out to him at the synod of Quierzy. But there was more than resentment. Gottschalk used the expression long before Hincmar was concerned about its orthodoxy. He employed it in poetry, in the prayers he composed, and in his theological writings. Gottschalk took the expression for granted and did not explain it until the archbishop gave him a reason to do so.

Gottschalk's Poems

Gottschalk, it should be noted, has been recognized a distinguished place in the development of medieval Latin poetry:

> In the mid-ninth century we see for the first time the emergence of a fully fledged lyrical stanzaic form in a handful of Latin songs by Gottschalk, a monk at Fulda. These are set in the stylized mold of penitential hymns, yet there is a strong undercurrent of the poet's own fears and griefs, and in one song at least the transformation into a personal testimony is complete.[77]

Before the polemic started in 849-850, Gottschalk already associated *unus* with *trinus*. He did this in his poetry. An example occurs in his best known poem, *Ut quid jubes, pusiole?*[78] This is an elegiac complaint about exile, on the theme of Psalm 137.[79] The rhythm is Gottschalk's own. Each stanza begins with two lines in iambic and continues with four lines in trochaic,[80] the whole being haunted by the constant recurrence of one single rime in "e." Six stanzas of complaint about not being able to sing in exile end on the same line, *O cur jubes canere?* The next two stanzas celebrate spontaneous joyful singing, ending with *Hoc cano ultronee* and *Hoc cano spontanee*. At the end the poet turns to humility (stanza 9: *Hoc rogo humillime*) and to doxology (stanza 10: *Carmen dulce/ Tibi rex piissime*). It is in stanza 8 that God is called trine and one:

> *Benedictus es Domine*   (Blessed are you, Lord,
> *Pater Nate Paraclite*   Father Son Paraclete

> *Deus trine Deus une* Trine God one God,
> *Deus summe Deus pie* Supreme God pious God
> *Deus juste*   Just God,
> *Hoc cano spontanee.*[81] I sing this spontaneously).

Here the poet associates the words "trine" and "one" as jointly describing God. "Trine" is no more different from "one" than "supreme" is from "pious." Gottschalk's poetic letter to his friend and fellow-monk Ratramnus, written in leonine hexameters,[82] contains a similar formula:

> *Ergo hunc aequalem pariterque pium genitorem*
> *Trinum unumque Deum votis efferre per aevum*
> *Debeo supplicibus...*
> (To this equal pious Begetter, and likewise
> To the trine and one God I should eternally
> Bring my vowed supplications...[83])

Yet there was more than poetry in Gottschalk's poems. The association of *trinus* with *unus* as qualifiers of *Deus* was not due to poetic imagination or poetic licence. It proceeded from a profound theological conviction. God's oneness and threeness are inseparable. By the same token, however, the poet raised a grammatical and theological question that did not escape Hincmar: When may the concrete designation, God, be commuted with the abstract term, deity? The substitution of *deitas* for *deus*, the abstract for the concrete, raised the speculative question: Is deity equivalent to or identical with God?

Poetic Precedents

Whatever the underlying theology, Gottschalk could easily have argued from poetic precedent. The use of *trinus* to qualify the attributes of the divine nature had a long if not very wide tradition behind it. Gottschalk himself in the *schedula* cited Sedulius, who had spoken of *ternam...fidem*, *ternam* having the same meaning as *trinam*.[84] Yet Gottschalk was remarkably sober in appealing to his predecessors. He could have called more witnesses to testify in his favor on the basis of the poetic use of the adjective *trinus*. But he would also have found texts that could be quoted against him.

Already in patristic times Paulinus of Nola (353-431) had written: ...*Deus unus,/ virtus trina*...[85] Here *trina* qualifies directly a divine attribute and therefore indirectly the divine essence in which the attribute inheres. It could be rendered as "…one the God,/ trine the power…"

The ancient poet Prudentius (died, 410) also had written: *Est Tria summa Deus, trinum specimen, vigor unus….*[86] The noun, *specimen*, denotes the exemplary qualities of a model, or possibly the form or appearance of someone or something. One could say: "God is a high Triad, a trine model, one vigor…."

Nearer in time, since he was appointed to the see of Aquileia by Charlemagne himself, Paulinus of Aquileia (Patriarch, 787-802) was notably loose in his poetic use of *trinus* and *triplex*. The two adjectives seem to be interchangeable in his *Carmen de regula fidei*, a poetic version and history of the Christian faith:

> *Solus et ipse potens trinus persistit et unus.*
> *Personas numero distinguo denique trino,…*
> *In Trinitate manet sed subsistentia triplex…*[87]
> (He alone, almighty, perdures as trine and one.
> Hence I distinguish the Persons by number three…
> Yet in the Trinity a triple subsistence dwells…)

Before the deposition of Ebo, and presumably before 833, Walafrid Strabo had dedicated a poem to the archbishop of Reims:

> *Trina Dei vobis per saecula cuncta potestas,*
> *Aeternae tribuat vitae sine fine coronam…*
> (May God's trine Power for all centuries
> Grant you the crown of eternal life without end…[88])

In all these instances the line between oneness and threeness is fuzzy. Admittedly, the language of poetry need not coincide with that of strict theology. As Hincmar himself argued, when he objected to taking poetic expressions at face-value, poetry allows certain licences in the use of words. In addition, there are passages where *trinus* cannot possibly mean what Gottschalk reads in the term, where it certainly designates the multiplicity that corresponds to number three. This is the case in a poem of St Ambrose that Hincmar quotes in the relatively non-polemical context of his commentary on *Ferculum Salomonis*:

> *Omnia trina vigent sub majestate Tonantis.*
> *Tres Pater et Verbum Sanctus quoque Spiritus unum.*

Trina salutaris species crucis, una redemptrix...
Trina dies Jonam tenuit sub viscere ceti.
Tres pueri crevere Deum flagrante camino...[89]
    All triplicities flourish under the Thunderer's majesty.
    The Three, Father, Word, also Holy Spirit are one.
    Triple is the form of the saving cross, only one redeems...
    Three days held Jonas in the whale's entrails.
    The three children praised God in their fiery path...

Surely the parallelism of these lines makes it impossible to read *trinus* without the plurality of number three. The contrast of this plural meaning with the collective numberless plural of other passages clearly shows that the term could be used in diverse senses. Semantically Hincmar was as correct as Gottschalk. Yet each of them was deficient in not admitting the meaning that was the only one the other recognized.

Reversely, one may wonder if the theological dispute over *trina deitas* left a trace in poetry. Raban Maurus, himself a respectable poet in the tradition of Alcuin, heavily stressed the adjective *una* in relation to the divine attributes, essence, and deity:

Una trium essentia,	(The essence of the Three is one,
Una est et potentia,	One also is Power,
Omousion, deitas,	Omousion, deity,
Atque una aeternitas,	And one eternity,
Beatitudo sanctitas,	Beatitude, sanctity,
Magnitudo et bonitas.[90]	Greatness, and goodness.)

Since Raban was ignorant of Gottschalk's doctrine on the Trinity when he responded to Hincmar's query, this poem must have been posterior to the beginning of the controversy. The accent placed on *una deitas* and on the parallel oneness of all the attributes of God is likely to reflect an opposition to Gottschalk's *trina deitas*, prompted by solidarity with Hincmar rather than by deep conviction about correct trinitarian language. And yet Gottschalk's mark also is on the poem: *deitas* is listed among the divine attributes, along with *potentia, omousion, aeternitas, beatitudo, sanctitas*. Such lists of related or synonymous terms were in Gottschalk's manner of speech, not in Hincmar's.[91] In addition, the use of *omoousion* as a noun points to a deficiency that Raban shared with most of his generation in Francia:

He had not mastered Greek! Seeing *homoousion* as an attribute of the divine essence rather than a property of the Persons was in fact faithful to the later trinitarian councils, where *homoousia* was attributed to the divinity as such. But one may wonder if Raban Maurus the theologian, who admitted to Hincmar his own incompetence in the matter, knew that he was following Constantinople III rather than Nicaea I.

The *Confessio prolixior*

The strength of Gottschalk's conviction is manifest in the *Confessio prolixior*, composed, as we have seen, in 850, before the clash with the archbishop on trinitarian language and doctrine, to which it made no allusion. In it the monk explained and defended his interpretation of the Augustinian tradition on predestination.[92] While it does not feature the formula to which Hincmar will object, *trina deitas*, it closely associates unity and Trinity in its invocations: *trine et une domine Deus… trine et une dominator domine Deus… Domine Deus benedicta simul et invicta trinitas et unitas.*[93] In this context of prayer the expression *trina et una* also qualifies the divine attribute of wisdom: *trina et una sempiternaque sapientia.*[94] Similar formulations frequently recur in Gottschalk's trinitarian writings. They may have struck Hincmar as suspicious once his attention had been drawn to the hymns and to their defense by "some persons."

One may then surmise that it was the *Confessio prolixior* that first aroused Hincmar's interest in Gottschalk's teaching on the Trinity. This profession of faith is quoted in the second letter of Maurus, and there is every chance that Maurus was one of the first to receive it since he was the one who had brought Gottschalk to Hincmar's attention in the first place.

If the *Confessio prolixior* does not develop trinitarian theology, it opens an intriguing window on Gottschalk's attraction to the inseparable ties of trine and one, trinity and unity, and on his fondness for associating these words when speaking to God in prayer and of God in theological disquisitions. On the one hand the chief topic of the *Confessio* is predestination. On the other the *Confessio*, alluding to the oneness and the threeness of God, takes for granted that these do not constitute two different perspectives but only one.

The *Confessio* is essentially a defense and illustration of Gottschalk's conviction regarding the meaning and scope of twin or double predestination (*gemina praedestinatio*) in the teaching of the fathers of the church. Isidore "did not say 'there are two,' since there are not [two] but 'it is double,' or bipartite" (*non ait duae sunt quia non sunt sed 'gemina' id est bipartita*[95]). There are not two predestinations but only one, which is, however, twin. Predestination is *una quidem sed tamen gemina*: "one and twin;" *una licet sit dupla*: "one although double." Divine predestination is one in its source and twofold in its effects. Augustine compares it with charity, which, as love for God and love for the neighbor, is *gemina*, with the work of God which is both one and bipartite (heaven and earth), and with creation, which is quadripartite or quintipartite, yet is also one.[96]

A Metatheological Principle

One may understand from this approach that Gottschalk has discerned what he takes to be a fundamental law of God's action and being, namely, that at the two levels of nature and of grace oneness is compatible with and inseparable from a certain multiplicity. In the first case the one creation is of heaven and of earth; in the second the one predestination is double. And since God's action reflects God's being a further conclusion may be reached: In God also oneness is inseparable from threeness; threeness and oneness are one. The doctrine of the Trinity and Gottschalk's view of predestination converge. The connection of the two doctrines, however, is not made explicitly. It functions, as it were, as an implicit metatheological principle.

The *Confessio prolixior* correlates the joint adjectives, trine and one, with God and with wisdom (*sapientia*[97]), and it identifies God with "trinity and unity" (*trinitas et unitas*[98]). In other words, independently of any polemical intent, Gottschalk likes to associate these two concepts. When speaking to or of God, spontaneously or deliberately, the monk makes a close connection between unity and trinity. In the same mode of thought he envisions the divine attributes as being themselves directly affected by the joint unity and Trinity of God. In an *Opusculum II de rebus grammaticis* that is contained in the manuscripts published by Lambot, Gottschalk therefore prays the following doxology:

> Thee, Holy Trinity, thee, trine and one deity, thy elect always glorify. Thanks to thee, truth trine and one, the conquered falsity of rebels has ceased unwillingly.[99]

This way of speaking was not, one must admit on behalf of Hincmar, in the standard theological or liturgical usage of Western Christendom. But whether it was heretical or even wrong is of course a different question.

The Faith of Pope Pelagius

Had Gottschalk looked further for precedents in the theological tradition he could have found a papal formulation that was not far removed from the conjunction of 'one' and 'trine' that he so emphasized. The *Fides Pelagii* is a profession of faith of Pope Pelagius I (556-561). It is included in a letter, dated 3 February 557, that Pelagius sent to the Merovingian king Childebert I[100] (died, 558): *Credo igitur in unum Deum... Patrem ... Filium... Spiritum Sanctum... qui ex Patre intemporaliter procedens Patris est Filiique Spiritus: Hoc est, tres personas...; ut trina sit unitas et una sit trinitas.*[101] Composed as it was before the interpolation of the Nicene creed, the text says nothing about a double procession of the Spirit. Instead, the Spirit is professed to be

> equal to the two (*utrique*), namely to the Father and to the Son, coeternal and consubstantial, who, proceeding from the Father without time, is the Spirit of the Father and of the Son: that is, three Persons or (*sive*) three subsistences of one essence or nature, of one strength, one operation, one blessedness and one power; so that unity be trine and Trinity be one.[102]

Thus Pope Pelagius I professed the unity of God as *trina*. This was precisely Gottschalk's point: Since all that is one in God is also trine, then *deitas* is *trina*. Had Hincmar been acquainted with the writings of Pope Pelagius, he could have objected that in another letter Pelagius opposed the baptismal *trina immersio* in the name of the Three Persons to the *una immersio* of some heretics who baptized only in the name of Christ; and in this case *trina immersio* clearly meant three immersions.[103] The argument, of course, would settle nothing. But it would at least show that one person could, in different contexts, use *trinus* in opposite senses, that of Gottschalk and that of Hincmar.

Notes

[1] *Responsa de diversis* xvii.xxi includes several autobiographical passages. In one of them Gottschalk speaks of his "master Vuectinus" (Lambot, *Oeuvres*, p.170). This is Wettin, director of the monastic school of Reichenau, who died on 3 November 824. Before the Lambot edition, the poem was believed to have been written in an island of the Adriatic, after Gottschalk's expulsion from the county of Frioul, in 846, where his views on predestination brought him to the attention of bishop elect Noting of Brescia, who then complained to Raban Maurus; this is still accepted by Devisse (*Hincmar*, I, p.155, note 194). Peter Droncke esteems that 824 "seems too early in terms of Gottschalk's artistic development" (*The Medieval Lyric,* 2nd ed., New York: Cambridge University Press, 1977, p.236, note 1); he proposes c.850, "the poet's presence in the island of Reichenau" being then "only in memory." This is an acceptable possibility.

[2] PL 114, 1063-1082. He also wrote a poem about Wettin's death, 1082-1084.

[3] *Epistola ad Ratramnum* (PL 121, 367-372).

[4] I have not been able to identify Matcaudus; what Jonas of Orleans wrote about predestination is no longer extant; Lupus of Ferrières responded with *Collectaneum de tribus questionibus* (PL 119, 647-666); Ratramnus composed a *De praedestinatione Dei ad Carolum Calvum libri duo* (PL 121, 13-80).

[5] PL 107, 419-440.

[6] See above, ch. 2, note 4.

[7] In addition, Hincmar denied the validity of ordinations performed by Ebo when he briefly returned to Reims at the death of Louis the Pious, in 840.

[8] *Epistola* V (PL 112, 1530-1553).

[9] Laurent Theis doubts that the count of Frioul was literate; he suggests that clerics read the text aloud to the count (*L'Héritage des Charles. De la mort de Charlemagne aux environs de l'an mil,* Paris: Editions du Cerf, 1990, p. 84).

[10] *Epistola* VI (PL 112,1553-1562).

[11] PL 112, 1554B.

[12] *Epistola VIII synodalis* (PL 112,1575-1576).

[13] Janet L. Nelson, ed., *The Annals of St Bertin*, Manchester: Manchester University Press, 1991, p.67. The *Annals of St Bertin* are an

unofficial chronicle of events from 830 to 881. Prudence of Troyes was the author of this part of the chronicle. But Hincmar took over the chronicling of events when Prudence died in 861. He is likely to have added these lines to Prudence's text; Prudence did not share Hincmar's doctrine on predestination.

[14] *...si exhibuit fiomenta, si unguenta adhortationum, si medicamenta scripturarum, ultimum ustionem excommunicationis vel plagarum virgae* (*La Règle de Saint Benoît*, SC 182, Paris: Editions du Cerf, 1972, p. 552).

[15] *De tribus questionibus* (PL 119, 621-666).

[16] On the controversy on predestination, see Emile Amann, *L'Epoque*, 303-344; Devisse, *Hincmar*, I, 118-153, 187-280.

[17] Grundlach, *Zwei Schriften*, 258-309.

[18] *Sermo de praedestinatione* (PL 119, 95-102).

[19] *Epistola ad Godescalcum* (PL 126,84-96).

[20] *Epistola ad Godescalcum*, cited by Raban Maurus (PL 112, 1522).

[21] *Epistola* 129, to Charles the Bald (PL 119, 601-605); *Liber de tribus questionibus* (PL 119, 621-648).

[22] *Epistola ad Hincmarum et Pardulum* (PL 115, 971-1008).

[23] *Liber de divina praedestinatione* (PL 122,355-440).

[24] *Ecclesiae lugdunensis adversus Johannis Scoti erroneas definitiones libri tres* (PL 119,349-356). This has the form of an official statement from the church of Lyon.

[25] *De praedestinatione contra Joannem Scotum* (PL 115, 1009-1366).

[26] PL 45, 1611-1664.

[27] The five provinces represented at Soissons were those of Reims, Rouen, Tours, Sens, and Lyon (PL 125, 513B).

[28] In Latin, *Tucinum, Tuseum, Tussacum*, or *Tussiacum*, which has given Tusey in French: a royal villa on the Meuse river near Vaucouleurs (Meuse). It is peculiar that Devisse calls it the synod of Douzy (Devisse, *Hincmar*, I, 183). Douzy (in Latin, *Duciacum, Diciacum, Dotiacum, Duodeciacum*, or *Daziacum*), on the Chiers river, was the seat of another royal villa. Two synods met there in 871. I take these Latin denominations and the location of the two villas from Johann Graesse, Friedrich Benedic, and Helmut Plechl, *Orbis Latinus. Lexicon lateinischer geographischer Namen des Mittelaters und der Neuzeit*, 3 vol., Brauchschweig: Klinkhart and Bierman, 1972. More than forty bishops from fourteen provinces in four kingdoms (of Charles the Bald, Louis the German, and their neph-

ews Charles of Provence and Lothar II) attended the synod of Tusey of 860. Tusey was in Lothar's territories. The fourteen provinces represented at Tusey were those of Besançon, Lyon, Trèves, Reims, Sens, Cologne, Bourges, Tours, Bordeaux, Narbonne, Rouen, Arles, and Vienne.

[29] The synod of Savonnières, June 859, attended by forty-two bishops from twelve provinces, is sometimes called first synod of Toul; in some of the documentation the two synods of Toul are treated as two phases of one council.

[30] *Liber de tribus epistolis* (PL 121,985-1068).

[31] *Libellus de tenenda immobiliter scripturae veritate* (PL 121, 1083-1134).

[32] Devisse, *Hincmar*, II, 269-279; text in PL 126, 122-132 and Mansi XV, 557-590.

[33] PL 125, 69-474.

[34] The synodal letter was composed by Hincmar (PL 126, 122-132).

[35] Grundlach, *Zwei Schriften*, p.263. What this "presumption" was is not explained. There seems to have been no further polemic on this question between Hincmar and Gottschalk.

[36] MGH, *Epistolae*, V, p.487-489. The text is cited in Lambot, *Oeuvres*, p.11: *De his vero quod dixistis aliquos dogmatizare trinam et unam deitatem debere sentire et profiteri, unde hoc sumpserint ignoro.*

[37] Devisse gives the date as 849 (*Hincmar*, I, p.156) or "the beginning of the year 850 at the latest" (p.163); Jolivet (*Godescalc*) does not attempt to suggest a date.

[38] See below, note 54.

[39] This is council III of Constantinople, 680-681; Macarius was the Monophysite patriarch of Antioch.

[40] PL 125, 473-475.

[41] PL 125, 513B.

[42] The credal statement included in Rudolf's *Capitula* (PL 119, 703-726) features the formulation: *...credendum est... unam esse deitatem et substantiam et majestatem in tribus personis Patris et Filii et Spiritus Sancti...* (Cap. I, 702).

[43] This appendix goes from 615C to 618B in PL 125.

[44] Devisse, *Hincmar*, I, p. 157, note 208.

[45] Schrörs, *Hinkmar*, p.156; the writings of Gottschalk that have been published by Lambot were of course unknown to Schrörs.

[46] PL 125, 618.

[47] PL, 125, 615C: *statim in initio suae de trina deitate blasphemiae collegi et scripsi.*

[48] Devisse's proposed dates are as follows: 849-850 for Hincmar's first awareness of Gottschalk's trinitarian doctrine; 851 for the beginning of Hincmar's reaction; 853, after the council of Soissons, for Hincmar's ban of *trina deitas*; 855-857 for the redaction of Hincmar's *De una*. The date given for the ban (*Hincmar*, I, p.156) is certainly too late, since Hincmar clearly states that it was precisely this ban that provoked Gottschalk's reaction.

[49] "...the frivolities of Gottschalk, that were followed by the sheet from Ratramnus..." (Lambot, *Oeuvres*, p.11).

[50] *Miror enim prudentiam vestram quod istum noxium virum hoc est Gotescalcum qui in omnibus vituperabilis inventus est qui nec monachi votum nec sacri ordinis ritum sed neque predicandi officium legitime observavit scribere aliquid permisistis...Unde mihi bonum videtur si vobis ita placet quod supra memorato heretico nulla detur occasio atque licentia scribendi atque cum aliquo disputandi...* (Lambot, *Oeuvres*, p.12-13).

[51] Quoted in *Ad simplices* (Grundlach, *Zwei Schriften*, p.309).

[52] MGH, *Epistolae*, V, p.490-499; PL 112, 1518-1530.

[53] *De eo autem quod interrogasti utrum juxta Gotescalchi traditionem liceret trinam et unam deitatem et trinam et unam potestatem et trinam et unam sapientiam dicere miror quid velint dicere* (MGH, *Epistolae*, V, p.499-500; quoted in Lambot, *Oeuvres*, p.13).

[54] Devisse, *Hincmar*, I, p. 156, note 202. The hymn begins with the words, *Sanctorum meritis inclyta gaudia.* It ends with the doxological stanza, *Te trina deitas unaque poscimus/ Ut culpas abigas, noxia subtrahas./ Des pacem famulis ut tibi gloriam/ Annorum in seriem canant.* In the Roman breviary it was expurgated in the revision that was ordered by Pope Urban VIII (1623-1644), a Latinist and poet who wanted the hymns put into "better" Latin. Of this revision a modern liturgiologist has written: it is "now universally admitted to have been a great mistake" (Joseph Connelly, ed., *Hymns of the Roman Liturgy*, London: Longmans, Green & Co., 1957, p. XVII).

[55] The manuscript (Bibliothèque de la Ville, MS 83), discovered in 1930, is described in Lambot, *Oeuvres*, p.ix-xxii.

[56] Lambot, *Oeuvres*, p.130-179.

57 1. *Quid interest inter substantiam et subsistentiam? 2. Utrum Pater et Spiritus sanctus de divinitate substantialiter praedicentur? 3. De trina deitate et una, quae est sicut firmissime teneo et veraciter credo trina in personis una in deitate substantiae vel in unitate naturae. 4. De Spiritu Sancto aequaliter procedente a Patre et Filio... 5. Quomodo imago Patris est Filius...?*

58 The references are: I, Lambot, *Oeuvres*, p.81-91; II, p.91-93; III, p.93-99; IV, p.99-101;IV, p.101-130; *Responsa* 1-5, p.130-146.

59 Lambot, *Oeuvres*, p.259-279.

60 Lambot, *Oeuvres*, p.269, 270.

61 Lambot, *Oeuvres*, p.278.

62 Devisse, *Hincmar*, I, p.158.

63 Lambot, *Oeuvres*, p.96.

64 Lambot, *Oeuvres*, p.94.

65 Respectively, Lambot, *Oeuvres*, p.95 (*Ipsa nobis det exoro semper frui se trina et una jam gratis hinc vita et sit ipsi soli merito laus honor gloria sicut est ante saecula sic per saecula sit et in saecula infinita. Amen*), and p.99 (*Adiuvet nos perfectus trinus et unus Deus et dominus et verus et carus id est trina et una deitas et divinitas veritas atque caritas. Ipsi soli laus honor claritas. Amen.*)

66 Lambot, *Oeuvres*, p.96.

67 Lambot, *Oeuvres*, p.98.

68 See above, note 64.

69 Lambot, *Oeuvres*, p.83.

70 Lambot, *Oeuvres*, p.84.

71 Lambot, *Oeuvres*, p.90.

72 Lambot, *Oeuvres*, p.132.

73 Lambot, *Oeuvres*, p.132.

74 Lambot, *Oeuvres*, p.138 ff.

75 Lambot, *Oeuvres*, p.138.

76 *Attende et appende et sponte perpende... sperne contemne et semper... cave* (Lambot, *Oeuvres*, p.142).

77 Droncke, *Medieval*, p.32.

78 There are several variants for the first line: *Ut quid jubes...*; *Ad quid jubes...*; *O quid jubes...*

79 When was this poem composed? Gottschalk studied at Reichenau under Wettin in 823-824. The poem contains an allusion to Reichenau, but this could be a reminiscence. Droncke remarks that the early date accepted by other scholars, 823-825, seems

"too early in terms of Gottschalk's stylistic development" (p.236, note 1), and he proposes c.850. The date may depend on the identity of the *pusiole... filiole...* who is addressed by the poet. This young child could be the nephew who accompanied Gottschalk on some of his travels. The poet could have considered himself in exile (*exul valde*) when he was far from whatever he considered his home. The sea (*intra mare*) need not be a sea of water, but could well be, figuratively, a sea of troubles.

[80] F. J. E. Raby, *A History of Secular Latin Poetry in the Middle Ages*, Oxford: Clarendon Press, vol. I, 1934, p. 227.

[81] MHG, *Poetae*, III, *pars prima*, p.731.

[82] Raby, *History*, p.228 and note 1.

[83] MGH. *Poetae*, p.734; PL 121, 369A. The text could be read differently: "To this equal and likewise pious Begetter/ The trine and one God, I should eternally..." This, however, would identify the Father with the Trinity. It cannot be Gottschalk's meaning.

[84] PL 125, 479, or Lambot, *Oeuvres*, p.25.

[85] *Carmen* XVIII, verses 133-134 (CSEL, vol. 30, 1894, p.123).

[86] *Liber apotheosis. Praefatio*, verse 1, (CC, 126, Turnholt, 1966, p.73).

[87] PL 99, 467D-468C. The next lines should be quoted:
Non hunc esse Patrem, sobolem quam credo tonantem,
Sed hoc esse Patrem, summum quod germen adoro.
Et non qui Genitor Genitusque est Spiritus hic est,
Sed hoc quod Genitor Genitusque est Spiritus hoc est.
Virgine de sacra, sancto de Flamme natum
Credo Dei Genitum....

[88] *Ad Ebonem archiepiscopum rhemensem* (PL 114, 1108D).

[89] *Explanatio in ferculum Salomonis* (PL 125, 321D).

[90] *De fide catholica rythmo carmen compositum*, stanza 12 (PL 112, 1609-1621; MGH, *Poetae*, II, p.197-204). This is a long poem of six hundred lines.

[91] There were poetic precedents for long enumerations, e.g., the praise of Christ by Magnus Felix Ennodius (c.473-521), bishop of Pavia in 512/513: /*Fons, via, dextra, lapis, vitulus, leo, lucifer, agnus, / Janua, spes, virtus, verbum, sapientia, vates, /Hostia virgultum, pastor, mons, rete, columba, / Flamma, gigas, aquila, sponsus, patientia, vermis, /Filius excelsus, dominus Deus, omnia Christus/* (quoted in Remy de Gourmont, *Le Latin mystique. Les poètes de l'Antiphonaire*

et la symbolique au moyen âge, Paris: Mercure de France, 1930, p. 137).

[92] Lambot, *Oeuvres*, p.54-78; a *confessio brevior* preceded it (p.52-54). Devisse agrees with Capuyns (*Jean Scot*, p.10) that the *confessio prolixior* is most probably posterior to Hincmar's *Ad simplices* (Devisse, *Hincmar*, I, p. 132, note 80), since it is neither quoted nor specifically mentioned in *Ad simplices*.

[93] Lambot, *Oeuvres*, p.55, 76, 78.

[94] Lambot, *Oeuvres*, p.73.

[95] Lambot, *Oeuvres*, p.67; the reference to Augustine is to *In Joh. Ev.* (PL 35, 1531) and *De Civ. Dei*, VII,6 (PL 41, 199).

[96] Lambot, *Oeuvres*, p.67.

[97] Lambot, *Oeuvres*, p.73.

[98] Lambot, *Oeuvres*, p.76.

[99] N. 101, Lambot, *Oeuvres*, p.454.

[100] Childebert was the third son of Clovis, and the second of his wife St Clotilde (the first son, Theodebert, was from a previous concubine); he had a long reign of forty-seven years. The kingdom of the Franks was divided between Clovis's sons at his death, further divisions being prevented by assassinations.

[101] Pius M. Gassó and Columba M. Batlle, *Pelagii Papae I Epistulae quae supersunt* (556-561), Abbey of Montserrat, 1956, p. 22. The letter, called *Humani generis*, is n. 7 in this edition (p.20-25). Also in PL 69, 407-410, where it is letter n. 15. See below, chapter 10, note 20.

[102] ...*ut trina sit unitas et una sit Trinitas*...(Gassó - Batlle, p. 22).

[103] Letter 21, *Admonemus tu*, to Gaudentius of Volterra, in 558/559 (Gassó-Batlle, p.65-66).

Chapter 3
GOTTSCHALK'S *SCHEDULA*

The monk Gottschalk stood up to archbishop Hincmar on the matter of trinitarian language and doctrine. He argued from the theological tradition as he knew it. Yet, as is frequently the case in polemical writings, his memory of the Christian past was selective. His understanding of the tradition gave the past a slant that became the chief operative principle of his trinitarian construction. Gottschalk himself provides a good insight into what he took to be the heart of the doctrinal tradition on the Trinity. For the sake of an anonymous correspondent the monk of Orbais copied what Lambot entitled *Excerpta de trinitate,*[1] "Excerpts on the Trinity." The twenty-seven pages of this document contain texts that Gottschalk extracted from Fulgentius, Isidore, Fulgentius, Alcuin, Augustine, and again Alcuin. Clearly, he favored the recent tradition over the ancient: Alcuin is given more space than anyone else, and Fulgentius more than Augustine.

The thirty excerpts treat the following topics:

From Fulgentius (*De fide ad Petrum*):
1. *Deus* is the common natural name of the three Persons;
2. The holy Trinity alone is the true God by nature;
3. The three Persons are the one true God without beginning;

From Isidore (*Etymologiae*):
4. The word Trinity means "as it were triunity" (quasi triunitas), on the model of "memory, intelligence, and will," which in the mind are one, yet distinguished; "one is the same as three";

From Fulgentius again (*De fide ad Petrum*):
5. Father, Son, and Holy Spirit must not be confused or identified (This is the longest single excerpt);

From Alcuin (*De fide sanctae trinitatis*):
6. The three are one as God substantially and eternally;
7. Father and Son are not different in substance;
8. The Holy Spirit is common to the Father and the Son;
9. The Father is unbegotten and begetting, the Son begotten: they

are in each other without confusion (*alter in altero*); the Spirit
must be said to proceed from the Father and the Son, faith being
protected (*salva fide*);

10. Father and Son act jointly, the Father acting through the Son;
11. Father and Son are one life;

From Augustine (*De trinitate*):
12. The three are of one substance;
13. God has many attributes, yet they are one and they belong to the
three;
14. The three are "one supreme origin of all things…".

From Alcuin again (*De fide sanctae trinitatis*):
15. The Son is said to be, as God, equal, as man, inferior to the
Father;
16. The Spirit is never said to be inferior to the Father;
17. The Father alone is not sent;
18. The Son has a mission;
19. The Holy Spirit has a mission;
20. The Spirit is fully God;
21. The Spirit is the Gift of God even in eternity;
22. The Spirit is given twice: from heaven and on earth by Christ;
23. The Trinity is of one substance;
24. The characteristics of each Person;
25. The Trinity performs the actions of the single Persons;
26. The Persons cannot be separated;
27. God is above all;
28. It is better to say that the Persons are equal than that they are similar;
29. The divinity is everywhere entire (*tota*);
30. God is not in saints as in sinners.

This choice of texts reveals a prevailing preoccupation. The numerous references to oneness in substance or nature (items 1, 2, 3; 6,
7; 12, 14; 23, 29) refer back to the Nicene ὁμοούσιος, which thus
appears to be central to Gottschalk's trinitarian thought. There are
also references to the way the divine Persons are distinct (5, 9, 15-19,
24), to the attributes and actions of God (3; 10, 11: 13, 14, 25, 27,
29, 30), to the Holy Spirit, including the *Filioque* (8, 9, 16, 19, 22),
and to Augustine's psychological analogy (4).

The *Schedula*

The most complete explanation and justification of Gottschalk's trinitarian doctrine are contained in the *schedula* that he himself sent to Hincmar, and against which the *De una* is primarily directed. Yet the archbishop also alludes to some trinitarian writings of Gottschalk that are otherwise unknown to us, and he quotes from several without identifying them exactly. Given Hincmar's stress on the *schedula* it seems safe to assume that this was the first piece in which Gottschalk objected in public to the archbishop's condemnation of the *trina deitas* of liturgical hymns. The shorter pieces, called *de trina deitate* or *de trinitate* by Lambot[2] were presumably written later to clarify various points.

The *schedula* is cited in full by Hincmar at the beginning of the *De una*, taking up three and a half columns of Migne.[3] As is not uncommon in the theological writing of the age, the plan, inasmuch as there is one, is far from obvious. Carolingian authors often write out of the abundance of their heart rather than follow a clearly organized sequence of ideas. Yet a pattern is vaguely discernible. I would distinguish eight sections.

(1) The text begins with considerations on the heresy of Sabellianism, in which those who reject the expression, *trina deitas*, can easily fall: PL 125, 475-476 CD.

(2) Support for *trina deitas* is found in the ancient tradition, specifically in the acts of Constantinople council III (680-681), in expressions used by Prosper of Aquitaine (*trina majestas*), Prudentius (*trina pietas*), and the poet Arator (*trina potestas*), in liturgy, and in the condemnations of Arianism on one side, Sabellianism and patripassianism, that Gottschalk assimilates to Judaism, on the other: 477ABC.

(3) The traditional doctrine on the Trinity is stated, and Gottschalk shows how this doctrine affects the concept of *deitas*: 477CD-478A.

(4) Further support for the banned expression is found in grammatical science: 478AB.

(5) The conclusion is reached: The stanza, *Te trina deitas...* is theologically correct: 478B.

(6) A long prayer to the Trinity restates the doctrine in doxological terms: 478BCD.

(7) This prayer merges into a review of arguments based on Scripture (St. Paul), on the baptismal liturgy, and on the recent poet Sedulius:[4] 479AB.

(8) The text ends on a plea to the archbishop to avoid Sabellianism and to follow the Church's true doctrine: 479BCD.

For clarity's sake Gottschalk's defense of *trina deitas* may be brought down to three major points. Gottschalk argues chiefly, (1) from the patristic, mainly oriental, tradition, especially from the acts of Constantinople council III, (2) from the analogy of faith, and notably from the baptismal liturgy, and (3) from the grammatical structure of theological language. On this threefold basis he assimilates Hincmar's doctrine to the condemned heresies of Sabellianism and patripassianism.

The Conciliar Tradition

Gottschalk appeals explicitly to the third council of Constantinople:

> It is time that those who believe and say that it is neither authorized nor true to call *deitas trina* should look up and read in the holy synod of Constantinople under Constantine the Younger....[5]

The council, sixth in the list of ecumenical councils, opened at the imperial palace "under the dome" (*in Trullo*) on 7 November 680.[6] It was attended by one hundred and seventy-four bishops and lasted for eighteen sessions, ending on 16 September 681. Gottschalk identified it as the council where "the Arians were rightly condemned and anathematized by one hundred and fifty fathers."[7] Yet the council of the one hundred and fifty is, traditionally, Constantinople I, held in 381 under the emperors Gratian and Theodosius I. It endorsed the decisions of Nicaea, confirmed the condemnation of Arianism, and formulated the creed that is still in use in most Christian Churches. Yet it is the council of 680-681 that Gottschalk has in mind. His main point refers to the use of the word τριθεοτεία ("trideity") in the document by which Constantine IV promulgated the conciliar decisions.[8] Of course the accepted number of attendants at councils may be more legendary than strictly accurate. But this was not Gottschalk's concern. And in any case historical accuracy was not one of his major qualities, even when he argued from tradition. This is manifest in his treatment of the sixth council, Constantinople III.

This council dealt chiefly with the condemnation of monotheletism, the christological theory that the incarnate Word has "one will" only, the divine will. The human nature of Christ was thus mutilated, deprived of a will of its own. This appeared to be a mitigated form of monophysitism, already condemned by the councils of Chalcedon and Constantinople II. Gottschalk, however, identifies the main achievement of Constantinople III as the condemnation of a late form of Arianism, in which he professes to find a kind of polytheism. The Arians, he says, were condemned because they "worshipped *tritheoteia*, that is, three deities."[9] Yet, Gottschalk argues, the Arians' improper use of the word τριθεοτεία does not rule out a proper use. As he finds it in the emperor's edict that is included in the acts of the council of 553 Gottschalk translates it, *trina deitas*, "trine deity." Thus, he maintains, even without the addition of *una*, the expressions, τριθεοτεία, *trina deitas* do express the Catholic doctrine. If the Arians teach that there are "three majesties, three pieties, three powers, three gods, and three deities," Catholics confess one divine majesty, piety, or power, one God and one deity. In so doing they believe that each is also trine.

Sabellians and patripassians were condemned, Gottschalk continues, because "in keeping with Judaic poverty (*Judaicam paupertatem*) [they] adore majesty, piety, power, holiness, deity, [as] singularly solitary and personally one."[10] Between the Sabellians' impoverished concept of God, that has been carried over from the Old Testament and Judaism, and the multiplicity that brings Arians to a form of polytheism, the Catholic faith professes the richness of the true deity: God is "naturally one and personally trine" (*naturaliter unus et personaliter trinus*).

Here is precisely the heart of Gottschalk's understanding of trinitarian doctrine: If God is naturally one and personally trine, so is everything that God is. The divinity and all the divine attributes are naturally one and personally trine. Among these divine attributes Gottschalk cites holiness,[11] majesty, piety, and power.[12] He adds that since "God-Trinity [*Deus Trinitas*] is the prime power,"[13] the divine power is naturally one and personally trine.[14]

The Analogy of Faith
Gottschalk does not use the phrase, analogy of faith. Yet this expression describes exactly what he searches for when he looks through several fields of Christian doctrine and experience where one thing is

also more than one. Such a field is, according to the *schedula*, the liturgy of baptism:

> When we are baptized, that is, bathed, we are certainly immersed three times. Yet for that reason immersion is trine, baptism is trine, that is, the bath is trine. There are not three immersions, three baths, or three baptisms. There is totally (*generaliter*) one immersion, one bath, that is, one baptism....[15]

Gottschalk's point is clear: the threefold immersion of baptism should not be counted as three immersions. It is not one rite among others in the baptismal ritual. Rather, immersion in water — the bath — is baptism. As there is one baptism, not three, so there is one immersion, not three. In this one immersion the neophyte is plunged three times into water. Hence the conclusion: the one immersion is at the same time trine.

This line of argumentation recurs a number of times in Gott-schalk's writings. Arator provides timely support, since he wrote that, like *potestas*, baptism is trine.[16] Again, *Opusculum II de rebus grammaticis*, a collection of somewhat disparate notes, lists a number of items where unity coincides with multiplicity: predestination is *gemina*, one in origin and twofold in its effects; Peter denied the Lord three times, yet in one denial, and he confessed three times his unique love of Christ; God has not three voices, but one that is trine; "and there is a trine immersion of baptism yet one baptism, although one is in water and the Holy Spirit, another without water in the Holy Spirit and fire, and another in martyrdom."[17] The one Paraclete is given three times; one seed falls into four terrains; one alphabet exists in four languages, Hebrew, Greek, Latin, and Chaldaean.[18]

As Gottschalk explains to a "prudent" and "blessed reader" the ten meanings of the word, redemption, he remarks: "Every Christian has been baptized, that is, bathed in a trine immersion." Likewise, the Father, the Son, and the Spirit are distinct divine Persons, each of which "is the naturally one and personally trine God, Lord, and Spirit, although each Person by itself (*per se*) is undoubtedly God, Lord, and Spirit."[19] The trinitarian imagery of baptism is even richer than this. For the Lord, who baptized the apostles with water, also promised them a baptism "with the Holy Spirit and fire." Yet all this makes only one baptism. Hence a further stress on the trinitarian analogy:

"Much more is God-Trinity believed to be naturally (*naturaliter*) one God, one Lord, and one Spirit...." This particular document concludes on a formula that seems to refer to a colleague in the monastic life: "This is the entire thing in question; therefore not once but frequently should your Most Cautious Fraternity be exhorted, along with all the others who do not reject me from their own. Amen."

The liturgical argument is also scriptural, for Gottschalk refers to Ephesians 4,5: "One Lord, one faith, one baptism."[20] And the biblical verse in turn evokes another analogy, borrowed from Sedulius Scotus. Faith is called trine in the following verse: *Iste fidem ternam ast hic non amplectitur unam* ("But the one trine faith here he does not embrace"). Gottschalk does not develop the point. Presumably, the one faith of Eph 4,5 is trine in that it believes in the trine deity.

Other analogies are adduced by Gottschalk, notably in *De trina deitate*-I. Thus, Adam, Eve, and Abel were respectively "created by God from the dust of the earth and from no human,...created by God from Adam,...created by God, seeded by Adam, and born from Eve."[21] Each of them being "perfectly human," Adam is "male humanity created by God from no human," Eve is "female humanity created by God from this man," Abel is "humanity created by God, seeded by Adam, born from Eve." Yet taken together the three of them constitute, "not three humanities, but one humanity that is triple (*triplex*)." They are then "greater and better" than one of them alone. Likewise the humanity of Peter, Paul, and John is one yet triple ("crucified,...beheaded,...resting in the tomb"). It is greater and better than each of them alone. In God, however, there is no triplicity. "God as total Trinity is not greater or better than each Person from the Trinity (*persona ex trinitate*)." Therefore *trinus* is acceptable, but *triplex* is not: "The trine God is not to be called triple."

Gottschalk argues that a similar coexistence of one and more than one is commonly assumed in theological language. One speaks properly of "Christ and his Church, as head and body, bridegroom and bride,...one person."[22] And the liturgy of the mass includes a triple *sanctus* at the end of the preface.

Theological Language

The argument that Gottschalk elicits from the triple *sanctus* of the preface is inspired by the Greek language. Yet, like Hincmar, and unlike their Irish contemporaries, Sedulius Scotus and Joannes Scotus

Eriugena, Gottschalk has not mastered Greek. While he notes that the triple *sanctus* is commonly referred to, in Greek, as *trisagion*, Gottschalk treats *trisagion* as if it were an appellation for God, that he renders in Latin, *trina sanctitas*, "trine holiness."[23] At this point Hincmar will have no difficulty pointing out that *trisagion* does not mean *trina sanctitas*, but *ter sanctus*, "three times holy," which is in fact nearer to the *sanctus sanctus sanctus* of the liturgy, itself a mere copy of the Hebrew superlative.

Gottschalk shared with the culture of his time a great interest in grammar, to which he devoted several *opuscula*. Grammar is more than an agreed way of combining words, themselves symbolic sounds, phonemes, into meaningful sentences. To the Carolingian mind grammar opens a metaphysical perspective. It is assumed that language and reality, grammar and being, are in strict correspondence. The forms of grammar copy the forms of creation. On the one hand therefore, just as there is one alphabet in Hebrew, Chaldaean, Greek, and Latin, so the grammars of all languages are fundamentally identical. On the other hand, grammar is the gate of metaphysics: the way things are said is the way they are. Gottschalk's incidental remark on *trisagion* has therefore an underlying depth which scarcely surfaces in the few words devoted to this point in the *schedula*. Yet there are relevant developments on the metaphysical question in *De trina deitate* IIIa and IIIb, in *Responsa de diversis* iii, and in *De trinitate* IV.

The starting point is linguistic: Can an abstract term designate a concrete being? Is an adjective the equivalent of the abstract substantive that names the virtue to which it corresponds? Gottschalk answers in the affirmative. For, he argues, the highest degree of being holy belongs to holiness as such. To affirm that God is holy amounts to saying that God is holiness itself. A similar reasoning is applied to all the attributes of God. God is holy, not relatively but absolutely, at the highest degree. It follows that God is each and all of the divine attributes at the highest degree: absolute holiness, absolute purity, simplicity, majesty, piety, verity, charity, power. Reversely, each attribute is identical with God. And since each belongs in full, like deity itself, to each of the three Persons, it is proper to say that the divine attributes, like the divine nature, are trine as well as one.

Gottschalk does not thereby reduce deity to the level of a divine attribute.[24] What he does is the reverse. His argument does not start from the oneness of God, that would then be seen as an attribute of divine being. Rather, looking at the many attributes of God, Gottschalk perceives that they pertain to the divine being, and thereby to each of the Persons. Because they share the divine oneness and threeness the attributes are one and trine. And so is the divinity in which they inhere. Since God is deity and is one and trine, deity is one and trine. Like the deity to which they pertain, all the divine attributes are essentially or naturally one and personally trine. In this Gottschalk, as we have seen, could have claimed the support of Pope Pelagius.[25]

Biblical and Patristic Arguments

In *De trina deitate*-IIIa, Gottschalk finds his own line of thought supported by Scripture. If Gabriel means "strength of God" and Raphael "medicine of God"[26] this is because God is strength and healing power, each of which is then naturally one and personally trine. Ruben is called by Jacob, *tu fortitudo mea,* "my strength:" this strength is one, yet also dual since it is both Jacob's and Ruben's. The angelic hierarchies have collective names that correspond to their perfection: Virtues, Powers, Principalities, Dominations, Cherubim (which means, Gottschalk points out, "Fullness of Knowledge"). Yet each member of these hierarchies is also, taken singularly, Virtue, or Power, or Principality, or Domination, or Fullness of Knowledge, and this to the highest angelic degree. But if singularity and collectivity are correlative among the angels, then by analogy they must also be inseparable in the Holy Trinity: "Because each Person by itself is prime Power, therefore Power is at the same time one and trine, and thus Principle (*principium*) is one and trine, and Fullness is one and also trine."[27]

In *De trina deitate-I* and in *Responsa de diversis-III* Gottschalk draws a similar argument from the fact that St Jerome calls a perfect man "perfection." But *excelsum,*[28] "the highest degree," is identical with *celsitudo,* "height."[29] The abstract name of a virtue thus properly designates the highest degree of participation in that virtue. Those who deny this linguistic principle fall, as Gottschalk sees it, into two errors.

Firstly, such a denial, the monk argues, implies a downgrading of God, for if God is not Trinity God is neither perfection nor perfect:

... he who denies *tritheotiam*, the trine deity, does not believe as he
should *mian theotiam*, the one deity...God would not be one, true,
and living, unless trine. I say why: because in this Trinity nothing is
anterior or posterior, nothing greater or lesser.[30]

The argument seems to be this: Since there is in God neither time
nor degree, everything that is in God must be the fullness of all that
God is. And, in this case, then everything divine, including deity and
its attributes, is naturally one and personally three.

Secondly, Gottschalk esteems that one cannot logically deny that
the abstract name of a virtue designates its highest degree without
also rejecting the Trinity and making God a quaternity (*quaternitas*).
But again the argument is not stated very clearly.

> Even if what cannot be had been or were, truly unless God had been
> and were, as he is, Trinity, God would not have been and would not be,
> as he is, undivided unity. For besides the three Persons that are alone
> good and entirely prompt and prone to have mercy on us freely, there
> is no fourth person who could be good. For God is not a quaternity
> but only a Trinity.[31]

God is not a quaternity, because the divine nature, being, divinity, or
deity — all practically equivalent terms — is not distinct from the
Persons, and therefore cannot be connumerated with them. Quaternity would introduce diversity between God and the Persons, and it
thus would destroy the divine unity. The argument is repeated and
slightly expanded in *De trinitate*-IV: The denial of the trine deity
opens up a sexternity, in that it necessarily divides each divine Person
in two, the Person and its deity:

> If deity is not, as I say, trine, then each Person is other than its deity,
> and thus the Trinity is six Persons, not three. But the Persons are not
> six, but only three, as Trinity makes clear. Therefore deity is thus natu-
> rally one and personally trine.

The Core of Gottschalk's Doctrine

Hincmar's *De una et non trina deitate* includes three long citations
from Gottschalk that come neither from the *schedula* nor from the
pieces published by Lambot. They are cited by Hincmar and com-
mented upon in nn. XV, XVI, and XVII of *De una*. Hincmar states

that nn. XV and XVI are taken from one document (*in eadem sua compilatione*[32]) and that n. XVII comes from another source (*inter alia heretica sua*[33]). But whatever their original location, which is unknown to us, XV and XVI unveil the heart of Gottschalk's theology.

N. XV defines personhood: A person is "what is one by itself" (*quod per se sit una*).[34] This is related to the alleged etymology of the word: *persona*, from *per se una*. In contrast, the divine nature "is nothing else than the general, common, and universal substance of the three; and each Person in the Trinity is nothing else than the proper, special, and individual substance and essence of the single ones (*singulorum*)." The difference between nature and Person follows from this: "In the nature the substantial generality, community, universality, unity of the three are shown; and in the Persons the individual specialty and propriety of each are declared."

This notion of personhood differs from the classical definition given by Boethius, which places personhood at the junction of individuality and rationality: It is "the individual substance of a rational nature" (*naturae rationalis individua substantia*[35]). Both Boethius's identification of rational individuality, and Gottschalk's preference for self-sufficiency as constitutive of personhood are quite distant from the approach adopted by Augustine. Without attempting to provide a formal definition of personhood, Augustine had written: Being is said "toward itself (*ad se*), person however relatively."[36] When therefore we speak of three divine Persons we mean that they are *ad invicem*, "[turned] toward one another, not each toward itself."

The difference between Gottschalk's approach and the Augustinian view is still more marked in the next quotation that is given in *De una*: "The personal names are by no means relative, but rather essential or substantial, like the natural names."[37] This clearly contradicts Augustine's notion that persons are *ad invicem*, relative rather than essential or substantial. Gottschalk however explains his point further:

> They differ only in this, that the natural names are equally common or general among the three Persons; but the personal names are proved to be proper or special to the single Persons.

On the surface this explanation seems to be at odds with another of Gottschalk's texts. In *De diversis*, Gottschalk has illustrated his

conception of divine unity by analogy with man. A man is both corporeal and incorporeal, exterior and interior. "The exterior Paul rests
in the tomb and the interior Paul triumphs with the Lord in heaven."[38]
Yet there is only one Paul, who is not "two men" (*duo homines*) but "a
twofold man" (*uterque homo*). All the more so in God:

> ...the Father, the Son, and the Holy Spirit, although they are spoken
> of in the plural because of their proper names, that are relative to one
> another (*propriis ad invicem relativis nominibus*), yet in their natural,
> common, and general name — God, Lord, Spirit — they are by no
> means spoken of in the plural, but as God unbegotten, God begotten,
> God proceeding at the same time, one God by nature (*naturaliter*) is
> known and demonstrated in all ways, for in these three Persons there
> has been, is, and will be — more, there cannot have been and cannot
> be — diversity or inequality or the smallest dissimilarity.

In spite of the awkward formulation of this text, Gottschalk's intent is clear. The relative names of the Persons — Father/Son, Fa-
ther/ Spirit, Son/Spirit — are not denied. What is affirmed is that
these relative names are also essential or substantial. Being personal
they must be essential, since the divine Person designated by the name
is identically the divine *ousia*, essence, or being. In God, Person and
being are not separated. Each divine Person is the totality of the divine nature or deity. For this reason deity should be called one and
trine.

The *schedula* contains no similar passage. That Gottschalk was aware
of the discrepancy of his vocabulary with that of Augustine can hardly
be doubted, for he was generally well informed of the Augustinian
tradition and he was in other ways a convinced follower of the bishop
of Hippo. One may presume that he did not wish to draw attention
to this discrepancy in a text that would be read by his archenemy. In
addition, the passage quoted in *De una* may have been taken from a
private letter to one of the monk's sympathizers. Hincmar was not
above having such letters intercepted; and in any case the line between private correspondence and the public domain remained universally vague before the invention of printing.

The Theology of Joannes Scotus

We will now make a detour through the theology of the only one
of the Carolingian theologians who was protected from some elemen-

tary mistakes by his knowledge of the Greek language. Joannes Scotus was well versed in Greek thought and especially fond of Platonic philosophy and of its use in the mystical theology of Denys. He was at the same time a powerful dialectician and insisted, in writing on predestination, that answering a theological question requires an operation in four points, that he called diairetic, oristic, apodeictic, analytic, or, in Latin, *divisoria, definitiva, demonstrativa, resolutiva.*[39] We may call them division, definition, demonstration, resolution. When Pardulus of Laon,[40] Hincmar's friend and devoted supporter, appealed to Joannes Scotus in the controversy over predestination, he and Hincmar were astonished that the most famous theologian of the period, who sided indeed against Gottschalk and any theory of double predestination, held a position that was quite different from their own.

Had Hincmar and Pardulus been more subtle philosophers they might not have been so surprised. Joannes Scotus's Platonism and his knowledge of Greek led him to use language and to adopt theological positions that were largely unfamiliar to Westerners, and not only in the matter of predestination. His most famous publication, *De divisione naturae*, a long treatise in four books in the form of a dialogue between a disciple and his teacher, designated both God and creatures, and even non-existent beings, with the one term, *natura*, this being "a general name for everything that is and everything that is not."[41] Much of the *De divisione naturae* explored the commonalty of all that is and that is not. In this perspective God is Trinity, Father, Son, and Spirit; and so is the human creature, endowed with "intellect, reason, and sense."[42] Correspondences between the eternal and the creaturely are grounded in the fact that it is in and through the Son, God's *Verbum* or intellective Word, that all is created. The eternal Word indeed is "the one form of all spirits, rational and intellective."[43] In the Scot's vocabulary, humans are rational spirits, angels intellective spirits. And the term, form, has a Platonic, not an Aristotelian meaning. The Word, *Verbum, Logos*, is the eternal archetype of every creature, "the Wisdom in which all who are wise participate."[44]

The Superessential Trinity

Trinitarian doctrine is at the center of this theology of participation. One participates in the three divine Persons through being (the Father), thought (the Word), and action (the Spirit). Because there can be no accidents in God, the generation of the divine Word and the creation of all things in the Word must be coeternal. It follows that all creatures have an eternal being or *ousia* in God. Furthermore, "Whatever in the creatures is apprehended as truly good and truly beautiful and lovable is [the Word] himself. Just as there is no essential good, so there are no essential beauty and loveliness, expect himself alone."[45] As he applied these notions to the debate over predestination between Hincmar and Gottschalk, Joannes Scotus could only conclude that everything is predetermined in the divine Word according to God's eternal thought and will.

In this essentialist perspective "one cannot deny that such names, Father and Son, are relative, not substantive."[46] Yet it is not enough to make affirmations about God and the creature's participation in God. For the human powers of affirmation soon reach their limit. Affirmative or "cataphatic" theology does not do away with the necessity of negative or "apophatic" theology:[47] God is not what we think he is. In fact neither negation nor affirmation is adequate, for God is still other than whatever they indicate. God "is essence, this is affirmation; non-essence, this is *abdicatio*; superessential, this is at the same time affirmation and *abdicatio*."[48] In this context *abdicatio* can only mean renunciation to affirm, negation. Both the way of affirmation, cataphatic theology, and that of negation, apophatic theology, must eventually be transcended in a language that is neither affirmative nor negative, but symbolic. As Joannes Scotus remarks regarding the knowledge of God that is available in this life, it is only through God-given theophanies, "divine manifestations,"[49] images, that one knows God truly as Trinity.

As he unfolded his trinitarian speculation Joannes Scotus tried to be faithful to a double heritage. Alone among his contemporaries in Francia he chose to echo the language of the Greeks while also reflecting the Augustinian tradition. The tension is unmistakable. But it can be mitigated by a better knowledge of the Greek vocabulary. Joannes Scotus tried to acquaint his readers with its nuances.

The Greeks speak of "*ousia*, essence, and hypostasis, substance. By *ousia* they understand this unique and simple nature of the divine goodness, by hypostasis the proper and individual substance of the single Persons."[50] By contrast, Augustine and the Latin fathers refer to "one substance in three Persons, meaning the oneness of divine nature with the word substance, and the trine property of the divine substances with the words, three Persons." Indeed, "the modern Greeks accept it, since they say *mian hypostasin*, one substance, and *tria prosopa*, three Persons." Joannes Scotus concludes: "All have one and the same faith, though diversity is seen in the meanings... The Father stands (*substat*) through himself, the Son stands, the Holy Spirit stands, and the three substances stand in one essence, for the three are one."[51]

The tension between the Greek and Latin perspectives can be softened by awareness of the utter transcendence of everything divine. "From the excellence of its essence and wisdom the holy and indivisible Trinity infinitely transcends the abyss of created" essence and wisdom.[52] When Scripture speaks of the womb of God one should "understand the secret bosom of the Father's *substantia*, from which the only-begotten Son, who is the Father's Word, is born, from which he is always being born, and in which, as he is always being born, he always remains... .He is not separated from the Father, for he is eternally and unchangeably in the Father."[53] The Word's eternal birth from the Father radiates with "the splendors of the saints," which are "knowledges of the elect and substantial predestinations in the Word of God who, as the apostle testifies, predestined us to the kingdom..." This happened *ante tempora saecularia*, "before the times of the world," in "the eternal times" that are identical with "the coessential eternity of the Father and the Son and the Holy Spirit..."

The generation of the divine Word and the creation of all things in him coincide. Yet this does not make the generation of the Son comprehensible. To creatures it remains unknowable and ineffable:

> No one among men or among the heavenly spirits can know the Word's generation from the Father... Only the Begetter knows what or who is begotten and how what is begotten is begotten; and the Begetter knows himself and what he is, and how and in what way he has begotten what he has begotten. Likewise, the Begotten one knows himself and what he is, and how and in what way he has been begotten; and he also knows his Begetter, and who and what he is. If indeed no one knows the Father except the Son and the one to whom the Son wants to reveal him, does it not follow that no one knows the Son except the Father and the one to whom the Father wants to reveal him?[54]

The Procession of the Spirit

Concerning the Spirit Joannes Scotus writes: "The begetting and sending deity precedes the begotten deity and the deity that proceeds from (*ex*) the begetting and the begotten."[55] The *pre*cession is onto-logical, not chronological. And the *pro*cession can be taken to corre-spond in some way to Augustine's *Filioque*. Yet Joannes Scotus also writes: "The gifts that [the Spirit] distributes are not his only but are of the Father from [*EX*] whom he proceeds, and of the Son, from [*A*] whom and through [*PER*] whom he proceeds."[56] As the equivalent of the Greek EK, *EX* connotes total origin from the Father. *PER*, corresponding to Greek ΔIA, designates the Spirit's origination through the Son, as in the doxology of St Basil. In addition, however, Joannes Scotus allows for an Augustinian version of the derivation of the Spirit: *A* designates origin from, without the connotation of to-tality that is implied in Greek EK, and that applies only to the Fa-ther.

Undoubtedly Joannes Scotus is by far the Carolingian theologian who is the most aware of the problematic dimension of the *Filioque*. In *De divisione naturae*, the disciple inquires: "If indeed the Holy Spirit proceeds from two Persons or, as the Greeks say, from two Substances, what is surprising or contrary to true religion in the be-lief that he proceeds from two causes? You leave me this obscurity. I hesitate." The teacher, describing what must have been Joannes Scotus's own dilemma, responds:

Indeed, indeed! This is a most profound darkness, which enshrouds not only you but me too. And unless the very Light of the minds re-veals it to us, the effort (*studium*) of our ratiocination is of no use to reveal it. The cloud of darkness is darker, in that the symbol of Catho-lic faith according to the Greeks, as handed on by the council of Nicaea, confesses that the Holy Spirit proceeds from the Father only [*solummodo*]... but, according to the Latins, from the Father and the Son, although in some explanations of the Greeks we have noticed that the same Spirit proceeds from the Father through the Son. Therefore, struck by the difficulty before the present question, I am carried (*allidor*) by opposite flows of my thoughts. I deliberate indeed what I should do in this question. Should we honor it by silence, since it is above the powers of our intent? Or should we somehow strive among us, insofar as the divine Light is reflected in our soul, to perceive [*intueri*], with-out temerity, what has been determined about it?[57]

Eriugena took the second path and attempted to lift the dilemma that impeded the agreement of Greeks and Latins on the procession of the Spirit. In a long disquisition he analyzed the notion of relation (πρоσ τι) in God, relation being the only one of the ten Aristotelian categories that is found in God, and he studied its application to the Father and the Son.[58] He then noted the special problem of the Spirit. *Filioque* presupposes that in God two causes, Father and Son, produce one effect, the Spirit. In creation, however, one cause often produces many effects.[59] Cases when several causes produce one effect are rare and, in fact, more apparent than real, for a chain of successive causes often conveys the false impression that these causes have acted jointly in the production of the final effect.[60]

Joannes Scotus draws from this an analogy with the procession of the Spirit:

> Although we believe and understand that the Holy Spirit proceeds from the Father through the Son, we must accept that the same Spirit has not two causes, but one and the same cause, that is, the Father, [who is the cause] of the Son being born from him and of the Spirit proceeding from him through the Son.... The Father, who is the principal and only cause of the procession of the Holy Spirit, is entire in the entire Son, as the entire Son is in the entire Father, from whom the Holy Spirit proceeds through the Son.... Thus the entire begetting Father is [*existit*] in the entire begotten Son; and the entire begotten Son in the entire begetting Father; and the entire begetting Father and the entire begotten Son in the entire Holy Spirit proceeding from the Father through the Son; and the entire Holy Spirit proceeding from the Father through the Son in the Father from whom he proceeds, and in the Son through whom he proceeds. And the three are one through what is understood as Trinity in Unity.[61]

In this convoluted sentence Eriugena affirms the Father as the unique cause of the begetting of the Son and the procession of the Spirit. The Spirit proceeds from the Father through the Son. But the Son is not born of the Father through the Spirit.[62] Furthermore, it is not from the essence of the Father that the Son is born and the Spirit proceeds; it is from the substance: in the Latin vocabulary, not from the divine essence but from the First Person.[63]

In any case, Joannes Scotus explains, the reality of God is infinitely above what creatures can perceive. The divine "Unity or Trinity is

not such as can be thought or understood by any creature or depicted by some imagination of whatever lucidity and verisimilitude."[64]
Yet in the contest between Greeks and Latins the Greeks have the
advantage. For, as is manifest in the works of Denys, they think primarily of creatures as being preformed in the divine ideas, "that is, in
eternal species or forms and unmovable reasons in which the visible
and the invisible world are formed and ruled."[65] This perspective
leads them to contemplate in God the prototypes and predestinations of all that is and takes place in time for purposes that only the
Father knows. Conversely, the creatures are seen as participating in
God.

This long detour through the Platonic theology of Joannes Scotus
Eriugena may now suggest where the monk of Orbais drew the notion, fundamental to his view of the Trinity, that since the divine
attributes are ontologically identical with the essence of divinity, they
may logically be treated like the divine nature itself.

Gottschalk's Source

Let us recall the dates of the trinitarian controversy. It started during the longer polemic on predestination, in the year 849. It continued until the synod of Soissons of 853, in which Hincmar vainly
tried to interest the bishops of the five provinces in the question, and
to obtain an additional condemnation of the dangerous heretic he
was pursuing. It goes without saying that the writings on the Trinity
did not stop the flow of ink on predestination. Precisely, in 850
Hincmar had to contend with the objections of a number of theologians and bishops to his minimalist view of predestination.

One event heated up the debate and introduced more confusion
than there already was. This was the appearance in 850 or 851 of
Joannes Scotus's *De praedestinatione*, addressed to the two bishops,
Hincmar of Reims and Pardulus of Laon.[66] Whatever the exact date,
Joannes's controversial contribution was posterior to Gottschalk's
Confessio prolixior that it quotes, and that was anterior to the trinitarian
controversy.[67] Now the view of predestination that was developed by
Joannes Scotus paid scant attention to what intrigued most of the
other participants in the debate, namely the relations between grace
and free will. Given the metaphysical and Platonic bent of his thought,
the Irishman was chiefly anxious to discern the status of predestina-

tion in relation to the divine essence and attributes. This was consistent with his preoccupation in *De divisione naturae*.

One of Joannes Scotus's adversaries, Prudentius of Troyes, reacted keenly against the Scot's contention that "predestination, prescience, will, wisdom, and truth" are the one divine essence and therefore cannot be, as Gottschalk says of predestination, *gemina*. Indeed, Prudentius maintained, the essential attributes of God — wisdom, truth, will — are, like the divine essence or substance, one. But there are also in God relative attributes, that would not exist without their relation to creatures. Such are prescience and predestination. Being relative to those it affects, predestination is manifold. Neither is it one nor is it the divine substance.[68] Prudentius rejected the notion that should predestination, a divine attribute, be twofold, God would thereby be two. As a relative attribute it is an action, and God performs as many actions as he wishes.

What is thus at stake between Joannes Scotus and Prudentius of Troyes is the divine oneness. How is the Creator's unicity compatible with the multiplicity of the created world? Whereas Joannes Scotus's Platonic philosophy placed multiplicity in the effects of God's one act, Prudentius saw God's actions already in the plural. In other words, God, for the bishop of Troyes, is not identical with the divine actions. The one divine will, an essential attribute, is God, and it brings about a multiplicity of effects, among which are the creatures and the predestinations of each and everyone of them. For the Irishman, on the contrary, predestination is in God and is God. One is reminded of the striking formula of St John of the Cross: *Obra Dios y su obra es Dios*[69] ("God works, and his work is God"). For the bishop of Troyes, however, predestination, a work of God, is not in God but in the creature, and it is not God.

Gottschalk of course rejected the notion of a single predestination. With the strict Augustinian tradition he affirmed a twofold predestination. But he did say and, apart from Joannes Scotus, he was the only one to say, that all the divine attributes are, like the deity, naturally one. He added that, by the same token, they all are personally three. Unlike Joannes Scotus, he did not count predestination among the divine attributes. He saw it, like Prudentius, as an action, a choice, and, against Prudentius, as a double choice, of the elect and of the reprobates.

Two points need to be emphasized here. In the first place, Eriugena
was himself a determined opponent of Gottschalk, even if he did not
share Hincmar's excessively elementary philosophy. Indeed, he called
the monk "a certain mucklover, the inventor and proponent of his
own heresies."[70] He unflinchingly addressed him as "heretic,"[71] caught
"in the delirium of your confessions or rather of your perfidies."[72]
Joannes Scotus did not show himself one bit more lenient toward
Gottschalk than Hincmar had been.

In the second place, the monk of Orbais was, in his view of God,
more subtle than his foes gave him credit for. Some of this subtlety
may even have been inspired by his critic Joannes Scotus. It is a rea-
sonable hypothesis that Gottschalk's basic thesis that deity and all
the divine attributes are naturally one had been learned from Joannes
Scotus himself. Admittedly, under Joannes Scotus's pen one does not
find directly Gottschalk's affirmation that the divine attributes are
personally threefold. In fact, however philosophical his discussion of
ousia and other terms that denote the unity of God, Joannes Scotus
always speaks of the Persons in a strictly biblical perspective: The Son
is born of the Father, and the Spirit proceeds. Nonetheless, without
using Gottschalk's vocabulary, Joannes Scotus comes close to his point
about the threeness of each divine attributes when he writes: "The
Father wills, the Son acts, the Holy Spirit perfects."[73] These are not,
he points out, three different actions, but only one act: "There is not
a will of the Father, and another of the Son, another of the Holy
Spirit, but there is only one and the same will, one love of the three
Substances of the one essential goodness, by which the Father moves
to make all things in Christ and to perfect them in the Holy Spirit."[74]

Here as elsewhere Joannes Scotus avoids the Latin term, *persona*,
and prefers to use the Latin version of the Greek word *hypostasis*.
This is of course, *substantia*. But this word, for most of the Latin
theologians, designated the divine essence or nature. It is no wonder
that Joannes Scotus's contemporaries found his vocabulary and his
theology confusing. Yet the Scot's position was after all not far from
Gottschalk's. What Gottschalk wished to emphasize with his controversial expression, "personally trine," was precisely the distinction of
the Three Persons. The Three share one divine action, which each
performs according to its unique character as Person. Likewise, the
Three share the very same attributes, each in keeping with its unique

relation to the other two Persons. In this sense, all the attributes of God are one and trine.

Indeed, Gottschalk could have remarked in defense of *trina deitas* that Joannes Scotus did apply this adjective to the divine causality in creation. In *De divisione naturae* the Scot confessed that he found himself in total darkness when he reflected on "the trine Cause of all things," *trina omnium causa.*[75] This Cause of all things, he wrote, is "trine and one, since the Trinity is believed and understood to be in the Unity."[76] The human mind can ascend to it by contemplation of causality in this world, as when "splendor proceeds from two causes, though it is understood to flow from fire through radiation," and thus "radiation is born and splendor proceeds from one and the same cause, and thus splendor proceeds from fire and radiation...." Passing on to the contemplation of God, one may then say that the Three Persons, each according to its divine personhood as Father, Son, or Spirit, are jointly causing the creature to be. So is the divine causality one and trine. Moreover, there also is in God, along with "one substance in Three Persons," which is the unity of the divine nature, "the trine property of Substances" or Persons.[77]

The Greek Tradition

Whether or not Gottschalk was acquainted with these texts, one important and generally unnoticed aspect of his theology emerges. The Saxon monk's approach to the doctrine of the Trinity was basically closer to that of the Greek Fathers than to the Augustinian and Latin tradition. It did not follow what is commonly regarded, with oversimplication, as the standard Latin method. His point of departure was not the one divine nature, on which basis one could investigate the threefoldness of Persons. Nor did Gottschalk seek for the divine nature apart from the Persons. It was not in itself, but in each Person, that he found the totality of the divine being, nature, essence, or substance. Such a fundamental orientation alerted him to the danger of positing a quaternity in God (one nature plus three persons) or even a sexternity (each person divided in two: itself and its nature).

The history of later theology shows that Gottschalk's fear was not unfounded. I am not aware of anyone slipping into a sixfold conception of God. But at the council of Reims in 1148 St Bernard (1090-

1153) accused the bishop of Poitiers, Gilbert de la Porrée (died, 1154) of finding a quaternity in God. Although Gilbert distinguished between the being that God is and the essence by which God is, he successfully defended himself, before the council and Pope Eugene III (1145-1153), from professing a divine quaternity. Later, however, the notion of a divine quaternity was condemned by the third council of the Lateran (1215) in the decree against Joachim of Fiora.[78]

The main point for the history of trinitarian doctrine is that the monk of Orbais did not separate nature and Persons. Everything of the divine nature, including divinity or deity and the attributes of God, was seen to be one and trine. And once the one divine substance or essence is trine, then it logically follows that, in reverse, each of the three Persons may be called essential or substantial.

The heart of Gottschalk's trinitarian theology lay precisely in his primary emphasis on the integrity of each Person, which is in itself the totality of the divine nature. His tragedy was that, being unfamiliar with the nuances of the Greek language, he did not, and presumably could not, develop a doctrine of the transcendence of the divine *ousia* and its primary residence in the First Person. The full expression of his profound insight into the richness of each Person had to rely on, yet also to depart from, the standard trinitarian vocabulary of the West, derived from Tertullian and Augustine.

Hincmar's Errors

We are hampered in our inquiry by ignorance of some of the documentation that was in the hands of the two protagonists. Each knew more of his adversary's writings than what he quoted from. Hincmar informs us that Gottschalk "compiled several *schedulas* of his blasphemies"[79] and "has written many other ridiculous things that we find among his disciples, to whom he fraudulently entrusted them for preservation."[80] Yet in spite of the loss of some documents the full scope of Gottschalk's deliberate opposition to Hincmar is sufficiently apparent. At the end of *De trina deitate*-IIIb, Gottschalk refers to "three heresies" that Hincmar has sent him.[81] This may designate three fundamental heresies that Hincmar espoused,[82] or three heretical propositions or documents that Gottschalk was invited to sign in exchange for more humane treatment,[83] or three letters received from the archbishop. In any case a reference to the archbishop's heresies fits Gottschalk's manner and tone when he confronts Hincmar: in his eyes the archbishop of Reims is an archheretic. But if Gottschalk does not identify the heresies with precision, he does give significant hints.

The first heresy is the Pelagianism of Hincmar's views on predestination. The second is the trinitarian heresy, that is formulated here in reference to divine love or charity, *caritas:*

> The love that the Son has is the Father alone, God unbegotten, charity unbegotten. The love that the Father has is the Son alone, love begotten. The love that has neither a begetting father nor a begotten Son is the Holy Spirit alone, love proceeding.[84]

In this context Gottschalk draws the line between Arians (there are three divine charities) and Sabellians (divine charity is personally one). In reality, divine charity is "naturally one and personally trine, as Catholics and true Christians believe and confess." Hincmar, however, does not confess this doctrine: if he is not an Arian he has to be a Sabellian. The third heresy refers to the consequence for Hincmar's own humanity of his denial of true divinity. Because he rejects "the true and living, one and trine, deity and divinity" Hincmar is "not worthy of being ever right, to say nothing of being a perfect man, humanity itself."[85] The archbishop is subhuman, a monster.

Gottschalk's Synthesis

The polemical angles of Gottschalk's anti-Hincmarian presentation has commonly overshadowed the depth of his trinitarian doctrine and its sources in the tradition. In the wake of Hincmar's judgment on his adversary, Gottschalk has been seen as a man who is excessively fond of theological novelty, who cannot brook any opposition, and who is unwilling to look at other points of view than his own. Indeed, as depicted by Devisse, Gottschalk is not only "intransigent,"[86] which he certainly is, but also a despiser of all human and ecclesial hierarchy, who practices a "free interpretation" of texts and doctrines and exhibits a combination of "egocentrism and theocentrism."[87]

Yet much in Gottschalk's disquisitions on the Trinity is entirely traditional. Gottschalk uses common and accepted images, such as the physical analogy of the sun, its splendor, and its warmth,[88] and the psychological analogy, dear to Augustine, of memory, intellect, and will. He also exploits the less common analogy of "two substances in each man, corporeal and incorporeal, visible and invisible, mortal and immortal, which do not constitute two men, one exterior and the other interior, but one man only."[89] Gottschalk follows Boethius in denying the distinction of essence and existence (*esse* and *est*) in God.[90] He firmly belongs within the monastic tradition that keeps together speculation and meditation. He never tires of insisting on the profound unity of faith and contemplation: One cannot "attain to the beauty of blessed contemplation unless one lives from faith in the immaculate truth." His explanations and even his diatribes are interspersed with doxologies, confessions, and prayers.

At the same time, however, Gottschalk's writings do contain instances of innovative language. The monk is not reluctant to pioneer new ways when he is convinced that they are orthodox. His non-relational concept of person is in his time unusual, since it is at variance with the theology of Augustine. The later theologians who will define personhood by incommunicability rather than by interrelationships could have appealed to his example.[91]

Certainly, Gottschalk was no respecter of persons. His style was never calculated to win over the archbishop. His fondness for redundancy could be irritating. He was needlessly prolix in lining up long strings of substantives, of related and sometimes more or less synonymous qualifiers, and of verbs whose chain traces out a sequence of actions. Not content with a sober mention of the presence of God he delighted in decorating it with numerous adjectives: "universal, unlimited, incomprehensible, invisible, admirable, great, and admirably powerful."[92] Examples of tautological repetition abound. This could be read as meaningless verbiage.

In contrast with this verbal superabundance, however, Gottschalk's arguments suffer from being extremely condensed. They are usually more pointed at than explained, more alluded to than expounded. One has the impression of a very intuitive person impatient with pedestrian reasoning. His theological prose wavers between prolixity in exclamation and affirmation, and brevity with density in explanation. Yet it is often subtle and delicate, as though Gottschalk's theology ascended, from time to time, to poetry.

Notes

[1] Lambot, *Oeuvres*, 101-130. Gottschalk's knowledge of the tradition may have been limited by the documentation that was extant in the monastic libraries at his disposal. Devisse's investigation of "Hincmar's libraries" (Devisse, *Hincmar* III, p.1467-1514) led to the conclusion that the archbishop chiefly used the library of his cathedral. But there is no information on what was available in the monastery of Hautvillers, where Gottschalk was in enforced residence.

[2] Lambot, *Oeuvres*, 81-99 (*De trina deitate*); 99-101 (*Item de trinitate*); 259-279 (*De trinitate*).

[3] PL 125, 475B-479D.

[4] Sedulius Scot was an Irish monk who settled at Liège around 848. Besides a number of poems he wrote commentaries on the epistles of Paul and the gospel of Matthew, and a book on political administration, *Liber de rectoribus christianis* (PL 103, 291-332).

[5] PL 125, 477A. This is the council of 680-681. The emperor is Constantine IV Pogonatos (668-685). The acts are in COD; Norman Tanner, ed., *Decrees of the Ecumenical Councils*, vol. I, Washington: Georgetown University Press, 1990; Rudolf Riedinger, ed., *Concilium Universale Constantinopolitanum Tertium. Concilii Actiones I-XI*, vol. II, *pars prima*, Berlin: Walter de Gruyter, 1990.

[6] Leo Donald Davis, *The First Seven Ecumenical Councils (325-787). Their History and Theology*, Wilmington, DE: Michael Glazier, 1987, 258-289.

[7] PL 125, 477A.

[8] The word τριθεοτεία does occur in several of Gottschalk's manuscripts (Devisse, *Hincmar*, I, p.162, note 238); others have τριθείας (Mansi, XI, 470) or simply ἡ ἅγια τριάς (COD 99-106).

[9] PL 125, 477A.

[10] PL 125, 477C.

[11] PL 125, 477B.

[12] PL 125, 477D.

[13] PL 125, 478A.

[14] ...*Deus trinitas potestas est prima*. For the Arians there would be three divine powers; for the Sabellians divine power is one alone.

[15] PL 125, 479A.

[16] *De trina deitate* I (Lambot, *Oeuvres*, p.88).

[17] *Opusculum II de rebus grammaticis* n.50 (Lambot, *Oeuvres*, p.471-472).

[18] The first two points refer to John 14,16 (the Paraclete) and Luke 8,5-9 (the seed). The third is more obscure. The four Lamentations are acrostic poems, each verse or stanza beginning with a Hebrew letter in alphabetical order. The argument assumes that the Lamentations follow respectively the Hebrew, Greek, Latin, and Chaldean alphabets.

[19] *Quibus modis dicatur redemptio?* (Lambot, *Oeuvres*, p.282).

[20] PL 125, 479B.

[21] Lambot, *Oeuvres*, p.81-82.

[22] Lambot, *Oeuvres*, p.83.

[23] PL 125, 477B.

[24] As suggested in Devisse, *Hincmar*, I, p.160-161.

[25] See above, ch. 5, note 101, and below, ch. 10, note 20.

[26] *De trina deitate* III (Lambot, *Oeuvres*, 93).

[27] Lambot, *Oeuvres*, p.94.

[28] *Responsa de diversis* iii (Lambot, *Oeuvres*, p.136); the reference is to *Commentarius in Isaiam* I, ch.20, v.20 (PL 24, 58A).

[29] *De trina deitate* (Lambot, *Oeuvres*, p.81).

[30] *Ergo sic et ego hic veraciter dico quod profecto qui negat tritheotiam id est trinam deitatem quia scilicet non colit unum perfectum Deum verum ac vivum qui negat Deum trinum quippe cum clareat luce clarius et sole splendidius quod non esset Deus unus verus ac vivus nisi fuisset Deus trinus. Dico quare. Quia scilicet in hac trinitate nihil est prius aut posterius nihil majus aut minus* (Lambot, *Oeuvres*, p.137).

[31] Lambot, *Oeuvres*, p.137.

[32] PL 125, 581B.

[33] PL PL 125, 588D.

[34] PL 125, 580B.

[35] *De personis et duabus naturis*, ch.3 (PL 64, 1343).

[36] *De trinitate*, bk 7, ch.6, n.11 (PL 42, 943).

[37] *De una* XVI (PL 125, 581BC).

[38] *De diversis* 10 (Lambot, *Oeuvres*, p. 311).

[39] *De divina praedestinatione*, I, ch. 1, I (PL 122, 358).

[40] Pardulus was abbot of Montier-en-Der when he was made bishop of Troyes in 848, by Hincmar.

[41] *De divisione naturae*, bk I (PL 122, 441).

[42] Bk I, n. 23 (PL 122, 568).

[43] Bk I, n. 27 (PL 122, 474).

[44] Bk II, n.3 (PL 122, 530).

[45] Bk II, n.74 (PL 122, 519).

[46] *De praedestinatione* I, n.13 (PL 122, 457).

[47] PL 122, 458.

[48] PL 122, 462.

[49] II, n.20 (PL 122, 557).

[50] PL 122, 613B.

[51] *Sub-stare* would literally mean, "to under-stand." Substance is that which "stands under" appearances. Hence its use to designate a Person, who stands under its own manifestation.

[52] II, n.20 (PL 122, 555).

[53] N.20 (PL 122, 558).

[54] N.20 (PL 122, 557-558).

[55] II, n.21 (PL, 122, 562).

[56] N.22 (PL 122, 565).

[57] Bk II, 31 (PL 122, 601CD).

[58] PL 122, 591-601.

[59] PL 122, 602-604.

[60] PL 122, 604-606.

[61] PL 122, 609CD.

[62] PL 122, 611-612.

[63] PL 122, 612-614.

[64] PL 122, 614C.

[65] PL 122, 615D-616A.

[66] PL 122, 355-440.

[67] PL 122, 366C.

[68] *De predestinatione contra Joannem Scotum* (PL 115, 1009-1366) reference, 1353.

[69] *Dichos de luz y amor*, n.106, in Simeon de la Sagrada Familiar, ed., *San Juan de la Cruz. Obras Completas* , 2nd ed., Burgos: Editorial El Monte Carmelo, 1972, p.138.

[70] PL 122, 358B. "Mucklover" translates *saphrophilum*, a term that John Scot must have formed from the Greek words σᾱπρία (filth) σαπρός (filthy, rotten) and φιλεῖν (to love).

[71] PL 122, 360C.

[72] PL 122, 366D.

[73] *De divisione naturae*, bk II, 19 (PL 122,553).

[74] PL 122, 554.

[75] Bk II (PL 122, 601B).

[76] PL 122, 609A.

[77] PL 122, 613B.

[78] As found in DS n.804; the reason for this condemnation does not seem to come from the texts of Joachim; yet it may have been induced by the illustrations of his texts, where the divine nature was shown as a circle, and the three Persons as three beams radiating from it.

[79] *De una* XIV (PL 125, 580A).

[80] *De una* XVIII (PL 125, 613B).

[81] Lambot, *Oeuvres*, p.98.

[82] Dom Morin thinks of "three heresies relative to predestination, concerning which Gottschalk had asked for the views of the most learned men of his time. Servatus Lupus was the only one who deigned to answer him..." (*Gottschalk retrouvé*, in *Revue bénédictine*, 1931, p.306, note 5). Servatus Lupus of Ferrières gave his response in his *De tribus questionibus* (PL 119, 621-666).

[83] *Sed jam tempus est ut tuas tres haereses quas mihi misisti et si eis consentirem omnem mihi humanitatem faciendam esse promisisti...* (Lambot, *Oeuvres*, p.98). Devisse (*Hincmar*, I, 159) sees the three heresies as three propositions that would have been contained in an exchange of letters between Gottschalk and Hincmar during the first phase of the Trinitarian quarrel, between 849 and 855-56.

[84] Lambot, *Oeuvres*, p.98.

[85] *Haec est vera ac viva una et trina deitas atque divinitas quam profecto quisquis scienter negat non est dignus ut sit umquam rectus ne dico perfectus homo id est ipsa humanitas* (Lambot, *Oeuvres*, p.98).

[86] Devisse, *Hincmar*, I, p.160.

[87] Devisse, *Hincmar*, I, p.158-159.

[88] *Responsa de diversis* 4 (Lambot, *Oeuvres*, p.302).

[89] *Responsa de diversis* 2 (Lambot, *Oeuvres*, p.310-311).

[90] *Responsa de diversis* 6 (Lambot, *Oeuvres*, p.308).

[91] Among these one should list William of St Thierry, John Duns Scotus, William of Ockham, and Jean Calvin: Tavard, *Vision*, p.74-77.

[92] *Responsa de diversis* 6 (Lambot, *Oeuvres*, p. 308).

Chapter 4
HINCMAR'S *DE UNA…*: THE STRUCTURE

The trinitarian theology of the archbishop of Reims is expressed in *De una et non trina deitate*, the polemical writing that was finalized in 856. However harsh its tone, the trinitarian quarrel was scarcely more than a parenthesis in the archbishop's dispute with Gottschalk over the question of predestination, and this longer debate colors his writings on the Trinity. The discussion of predestination was both pastoral and dogmatic. Hincmar feared the effect of teaching double predestination to those of the faithful who were *simplices et rudes*. Pastoral anxiety no less than zeal for orthodoxy dictated Hincmar's swift and determined treatment of Gottschalk at the synod of Quierzy. The archbishop was admittedly concerned also about truth, dogma, and tradition. But, on the strength of the canons and of the Rule of St Benedict, he felt sure enough of his doctrine to control Gottschalk with disciplinary measures. On this background, the challenge he received from the bishops of the ecclesiastical provinces of Lyon and Arles forced him to as thorough an investigation of the tradition as he found himself able to make.

The pattern of an authoritative disciplinary decision followed by extensive research in the doctrinal tradition recurs in the trinitarian controversy. Again the point of departure is pastoral. A hymn that contains false doctrine is misleading and should therefore not be used. Yet, given his canonical orientation and his monastic training, Hincmar was more likely to accept a liturgical tradition as he found it than to attempt to reform it. The hymn or hymns in question had been sung hitherto with no deleterious results. Even if a satisfactory justification of the formula were not put forward, the liturgical acceptability of *trina deitas* was manifest in its customary use, on the basis of the principle of Prosper of Aquitaine, …*ut legem credendi lex statuat supplicandi…*[1] Surely, as a monk and as a bishop Hincmar had himself sung this hymn long before he questioned its implicit doctrine and brought the weight of his metropolitan authority to bear against its liturgical use.

The occasion for the debate was furnished by the archbishop. But the debate itself was initiated by the monk's *schedula* in support of the liturgical use and the orthodoxy of the expression, *trina deitas*.

The ban on *trina deitas* was apparently not prompted by anything Gottschalk had previously said or done.

Hincmar's Hesitancies

There is ample evidence in the *De una* that after excluding the expression, *trina deitas*, from the hymnody of his diocese Hincmar went through a period of hesitation, not indeed about essential points of trinitarian doctrine or even about the wisdom of his decision, but regarding some more subtle questions of theology that were raised by the qualifier, *trina*. This hesitancy explains his letters of inquiry to Raban Maurus, the tardiness of his response to Gottschalk's protest, and the extensive researches in canonical and theological literature that went into the composition of *De una*.

The chronology is significant. Some time between the spring of 849 and early 850 Hincmar hears that some monks are defending an unusual trinitarian formula, *trina deitas*. The monks' agitation must have been kindled by some incident, but we have no information as to the nature of it. Hincmar also learns that Ratramnus has recently supported the orthodoxy of the expression. In 850 he receives Gottschalk's *confessio prolixior*, where the word *trina* appears in good place, with no openly polemical intent, as a qualifier of several attributes of God. Hincmar writes to Raban Maurus for advice, receives an uncommittal answer, and, suspicious of the expression, bans the singing of *trina deitas*.

Just at that time, however, Hincmar is painfully learning from the growing predestinarian controversy not to step too fast into a theological debate. In the spring of 849 he has obtained the condemnation of Gottschalk's doctrine on predestination by the synod of Quierzy. Yet precisely when he believes that the synod has correctly expressed the mind of the church, the archbishop of Reims belatedly discovers the difficulties of the problem.

Prominent theologians are taking their distance from him and from the synod of Quierzy. In 850 John Scot, director of the Palatial School at the court of Charles the Bald, condemns Gottschalk without approving Hincmar's doctrine,[2] and Lupus, abbot of Ferrières, leans toward Gottschalk's interpretation of St Augustine.[3] In 850 also Ratramnus comes to Gottschalk's rescue.[4] In 851 the deacon Florus leads the opposition of the church of Lyon to Hincmar's doctrine on predestination, which is assimilated to semi-pelagianism.[5] Prudentius of Troyes in 849 or 850 gives qualified support to Hincmar,[6] but he later shifts his position closer to Florus and Gottschalk.[7] In May 853 Hincmar's four *capitula* are endorsed by another synod of Quierzy[8] and is approved by the synod of Soissons. But in January 855 the synod of Valence, representing the episcopate of Southern France, follows Remi of Lyon and Florus, and directly contradicts Hincmar and the *capitula* of Quierzy.[9]

In 850 Hincmar has not yet run into the Southern bishops' opposition, and the predestinarian controversy is yet to reach its most uncomfortable peak. Yet the archbishop of Reims already has ample reason to be more cautious in a public discussion of trinitarian theology than he has been in regard to predestination. He proceeds to a careful inquiry, only to run into the paradox that the resulting volume, *De una et non trina deitate,*[10] leaves his contemporaries totally indifferent. Scarcely anyone is interested in the new controversy.[11] Ratramnus has publicly taken Gottschalk's side. But no one brings forth any argument in favor of Hincmar, even if the synod of the five provinces (Soissons, 853) has listened to him with respect, and Rudolf of Bourges has brought him a moderate degree of support. What was the reason for this massive silence?

The intensifying controversy over predestination may have had a numbing effect on theological minds in schools and monasteries. One gets tired of polemics. But this does not account for the whole situation. Hincmar believes that Gottschalk is a heretic on the doctrine of the Trinity, but he is the only one to think so. Either the other bishops and the theologians of Francia do not think him heretical, or else they do not care whether he is or not. In any case the question does not seem to them to warrant additional theological turmoil. The new problem between Hincmar and Gottschalk is seemingly more verbal than real. The other participants in the predestinarian dispute do not consider that the difference of trinitarian language is worth getting upset about.

Hincmar's Posthumous Failure

In addition to the difficulties he faced in his lifetime in regard to trinitarian doctrine, Hincmar has not been favored by posterity. Historians of doctrine have judged his *De una et non trina deitate* to be practically illegible! However mature Hincmar's trinitarian theology was when he composed *De una*, Catholic authors have generally been kind neither to it nor to the whole controversy. The nineteenth century historian, René Rohrbacher (1789-1856), who is most sympathetic to Hincmar and tells the story of the predestinarian controversy at great length, omits the debate over trinitarian language.[12] The very discoverer of Gottschalk's texts, Dom Morin (1861-1946), calls the whole polemic a "ridiculous game with words."[13] And Emile Amann (1880-1948) sums up the general feeling when he describes Hincmar's *De una* as "a work in which no one has been tempted to penetrate,… a mess where very few historians of theological literature have ventured."[14]

Protestant historians have been kinder. Adolf Harnack, who explains at the length the predestinarian controversy, mentions the trinitarian quarrel only in a footnote as a "noteworthy" instance of the monk's irresponsible behavior, for which he blames Gottschalk's weakened faculties: "The ill usage he had suffered seems to have rendered Gottschalk at times irresponsible for his actions in the last years of his life."[15] This suggests, however, that Hincmar's position on the trinitarian question, if not his treatment of the recalcitrant monk, was, in the main, correct. Reinhold Seeberg does not mention the problem of *trina deitas*.[16] More recently, however, Jaroslav Pelikan has presented both sides of the trinitarian discussion with sensitivity. Without entering into details he deems the debate to be "more significant… than that between Elipandus and Migetius" in Spain,[17] which, after all, is not saying much.

The Structure of *De una*

Admittedly the structure and the division of *De una* are by no means clear. Yet the book is not so indigestible as Amann affirmed. It is divided in a prologue — which includes Gottschalk's *schedula* — and nineteen sections. Each section begins with a quotation from Gottschalk, which is then refuted at length. The quotations come mostly from the *schedula*, but also, in sections XV to XIX, from others of Gottschalk's writings. They are marked, as Hincmar alerts his readers, by a symbol that is commonly used in Latin texts to draw attention to a mistake, the *obelus*: (÷). Hincmar's refutations of Gottschalk are marked by another conventional symbol, the *chrisma*: (XP).

Devisse divides the *De una* in six broad sections:[18]

I. A prologue with a general argumentation (PL 125, 473-483).

II. An orderly argumentation from Fathers, Scriptures, councils (483-510).

III. A parenthesis on the falsification of texts (510-528).

IV. Two series of grammatical studies, intermeshed with the next section (540-550; 565-572).

V. Two series of arguments from various texts, intermeshed with the previous section (528-540; 565-572).

VI. A largely repetitive section, that may have been composed at a later time (588-615 C): it "has much more disorder. Hincmar uses the same texts, the same arguments to refute new writings by the monk."[19]

By a strange oversight, however, columns 572-588 are not accounted for in this plan. One therefore should look again at the structure of *De una*. Before doing this, however, I will examine what is clearly the prologue or introduction to the book.

The Prologue

This stands by itself. It includes Hincmar's address, as "bishop of Reims and member of the people of God," to "the beloved children of the Catholic Church and our co-ministers," an account of the start of the controversy (473C to 476B), an explanation of the occasion of the book with an overview of its plan: Hincmar has been asked, presumably by some of his co-ministers the bishops, to provide the text of Gottschalk's *schedula* and to refute it point by point (476B to 476C). The text of the *schedula* follows (476C to 479D), after which Hincmar inserts a general introduction to the question (479D to 483D).

This introduction is destined in the author's mind to highlight the major importance of holding the correct trinitarian faith. It is in fact a remarkable piece of work, well organized and eloquent. It locates Gottschalk's writing in a broad overview of all the heresies concerning the nature of God.

Already in paradise, Hincmar explains, the devil tempted Adam and Eve to polytheism and idolatry. For that purpose he distorted the words of God in Genesis 1,26 ("Let us make Adam in our image and likeness") in a polytheistic direction. Taking the plural literally, the devil assured "the first humans": "You shall be like gods!" (Gen 3,5). But the true sense of the words was that "the nature or deity in whose image man was to be made is not trine but one: for in his image the holy Trinity, one God, made him."[20] In other terms, "God, in whose image man was made, is not one Person but three Persons." This is the teaching of Athanasius, Hilary, Ambrose, and Augustine. It contradicts two diabolical opinions, that of Sabellius, who "taught union in the trinity of Persons," and that of Arius, who "divided the substance of the one deity." In the saying of Jesus, "My Father and I are one" (John 10,30), Sabellius distorted "are" (*sumus*) and Arius distorted "one" (*unum*). And now Gottschalk, "the devil's own son," has followed Arius: he has "dogmatized a trine deity."[21] He has contradicted Ambrose and Augustine, from whom Hincmar cites two long passages.[22]

The quotation from Ambrose leads the archbishop to put forward his understanding of the word, trine:

> Hence it is manifest that just as unity has no number, so trine or trinity has number. Therefore in the holy and inseparable Trinity it is not the unity of the deity but the property of the Persons that receives [the adjective] *trinum* or *trina*, which has number.[23]

The quotation from Augustine illustrates Hincmar's contention that Gottschalk is a trouble-maker, "filled with a diabolical spirit, as we have very often experienced."[24] Surveying the history of the Church, Hincmar then remarks that the devil carefully chooses the moments when he will launch new heresies: these are periods of peace and quiet, when "many who could know and explain the Scriptures hide among the people of God and do not give the solutions of difficult questions because no calumniator has arisen."[25]

Yet, Hincmar admits, heresies are useful. When they spring up, "many things that pertain to the Catholic faith…are more diligently examined, more clearly understood, and more eagerly preached."[26] The teaching on the Trinity was not perfect before Arius, on penance before Novatian. By the same token many texts of Scripture have been clarified in debate: concerning the divine Christ against Photinus, the human Christ against Mani, the Trinity against Sabellius, the unity of the Trinity against the Arians, Eunomians, and Macedonians, the Church against the Donatists. This points up the incidental use of heresies for the advantage of the true faith. It shows the pastoral necessity of "condemnation pronounced by episcopal judgment (*judicium episcopale*), than which there is no greater in the

Church," and which God does use for the salutary correction of heretics.[27] Such condemnations should not induce despair: "We do not know what happens tomorrow: either before the end of his life one is to despair of someone, or it is possible for God to ignore the refusal of penance and God will offer penance and, receiving the sacrifice of a contrite spirit and heart, absolve of the guilt of whatever just condemnation, and not condemn the condemned."[28] Whatever anathemas have been pronounced by bishops, God may still change the heart of the condemned.

Hincmar is not unaware of the irony of the situation. Pastoral severity is required by our ignorance of divine predestination: "Not knowing who belongs, who does not belong, to the number of the predestined, we must be moved by charitable love to wish that all be saved."[29] We should therefore strive that all "who are justified by faith (*justificati ex fide*) have peace with God." On the one hand, "whoever will have been separated from the Catholic Church, however worthy of praise he thinks his life has been, by virtue of the sole evil of having been disjuncted from the unity of Christ will not have life."[30] On the other hand, there are evil men in the church itself; yet no one can be soiled by the sins of others. Hincmar concludes: "These remarks are enough in this preface concerning the words and sense of the Fathers;"[31] he will now "respond one by one to the deadly words of pestiferous Gottschalk."

Two points have been made clear. Firstly, Hincmar is convinced that he has uncovered a major heresy that denies the fundamental doctrine of the oneness of God. The remote origin of this heresy is no other than the primeval temptation in the Garden of Eden. Whatever God's endless mercy may eventually do in Gottschalk's heart to bring him to eternal salvation, the bishop's duty is to separate the erring and obstinate monk from the people of God.

Secondly, Hincmar is convinced that Gottschalk's new heresy threatens the church with polytheism and idolatry. This is partly a question of semantics. The term, trine, in Hincmar's mind, implies number and multiplicity. But this is precisely the archbishop's weak point. For Gottschalk constantly maintains the opposite. For him, trine does not mean triple; rather, affirming the three divine Persons, the word maintains oneness in the divine nature. Yet the question is more than lexical. The primary difference between Hincmar and Gottschalk lies in diverging approaches to theological language. As well as being a theologian Gottschalk is a distinguished if not very fertile religious poet. As a poet he feels free and willing to assign a special sense to the words he uses, and he expects others to read them in the sense he intends. Under his pen, trine never means triple; it does not imply number or multiplicity. This contention, however, Hincmar will not accept, in spite of his own poetic leanings.

Hincmar's Poetry

Like most theologians of the time, including his mentor Raban Maurus, the archbishop of Reims has composed respectable poems. His *Vita sancti Remigii*, a life of St Remi, his predecessor who had baptized Clovis as the first Catholic king of the Franks, included a poetic epitaph of thirty-two lines.[32] His other compositions include several epitaphs, one of which is for his own sepulchre, two inscriptions for an altar, a third for a manuscript of the gospels, a piece addressed to his nephew, the future Hincmar of Laon, who is then a "young priest," and a poem of one hundred lines in praise of the Virgin.

There was also a poem of four hundred and forty lines, *Ferculum Salomonis*, of which something may be said although most of it is now lost. According to Flodoardus, this "beautiful metric work" was composed in honor of Charles the Bald.[33] It must have been written around 854-855, after the start of the trinitarian controversy. The topic was the "throne of Solomon" of the Song of Songs 3,7. A dozen lines have remained, along with the dedication to King Charles.[34] It was accompanied by a commentary in prose that has survived, *Explanatio in ferculum Salomonis*.[35] Medieval commentators on the Song of Songs commonly related the throne of Solomon to the mystical life. Hincmar's interpretation was less individualistic and more ecclesial, though no less allegorical. The throne was one of many biblical symbols of "the church, the body of Christ, in whose unity anyone is incorporated in the same Christ by faith..."[36] This was, Hincmar said, the holy doctors' interpretation.

The prose text is not polemical; and its central concern lies in symbolic interpretation. Yet allusions to the current polemics are clear. Hincmar cites a poem of Ambrose in which the word *trina* evidently implies triplicity: *Trina dies Jonam tenuit sub viscere ceti*.[37] He not only affirms the unity of deity, but is also at pains to illustrate the coincidence between trinity and unity. To this end he guides his reader through labyrinthine considerations on numerology, about one and three, and also about seven, four, forty, ten, one hundred, the number by which "eternal life is designated,"[38] and more.... This leads, somewhat obscurely, to the conclusion that the temple of Jerusalem "was an image of the sacrosanct flesh of the Lord that he took from the Virgin, for she is equally his body which is the church, for the temple designated the body and the soul of each of the faithful."[39] This identification of the Virgin with the church balances Hincmar's identification of Eve with Adam: *et Eva ipsa est Adam.*[40]

In spite of its allusions to on-going polemics, the *Explanation of the Throne of Solomon* formulates Hincmar's doctrine of the Trinity non-polemically:

> ...in all things the unity of deity is in the Trinity of Persons, and the Trinity of Persons is in the unity of deity, because from the Father alone, that is, from the substance of the Father, the equal and consubstantial Son is generated, not created, and from the Father and the Son the coequal and consubstantial Holy Spirit equally proceeds, for he is equally God, wholly of the Father and wholly of the Son, for he is by nature one Spirit of the Father and the Son.[41]

The Structure of *De una*

Outside of his few poems and of an occasional exploration of symbolism, the archbishop of Reims remains a strict canonist, unbending in applying the canons as he understands them and seldom departing from what he has identified as the definition of a term. In this canonical perspective language is not private but social. It will be heard and read in its conventional signification, not in subjective and idiosyncratic meanings that may be assigned to it by poetic imagination. Whether therefore Gottschalk intends to affirm the authentic unity and Trinity of God is irrelevant. The point lies in what he actually teaches according to the obvious sense of his words: He divides the divine nature in three, and he thus posits three gods. In the long run the solution of the question depends on knowledge of the tradition. Has the tradition used the word, trine, meaning triple, as a qualifier of the one deity? While the bulk of *De una et non trina deitate* refutes Gottschalk's doctrine and arguments, it constantly presupposes the narrow understanding and use of language at the service of the trinitarian doctrine which the archbishop formulated in his *Explanation on the Throne of Solomon.*

Each of the nineteen sections of *De una* is opened by a short quote from Gottschalk, which Hincmar then refutes or at least to criticizes. As we have seen, Devisse identifies two main sections, I-XIV, dealing with the *schedula*, and XV-XIX, where other texts of Gottschalk are refuted. Yet the archbishop's argumentation becomes clearer if we divide the text in two parts, followed by two appendices:

— Part I is identical with section I (PL 125, 483D to 510D): The central thesis of Gottschalk's *schedula* is refuted.

— Part II comprises sections II to XIV (510D to 580A): Having destroyed Gottschalk's main thesis, Hincmar shows up the fallacy of a number of his arguments.

The rest of the book may be considered as forming two appendices, or, alternatively, a third part divided in two sections:

— Appendix I is made of sections XV to XVIII (580A to 613C): Hincmar completes his argumentation by refuting quotations he has culled from other works of Gottschalk.

— Appendix II is section XIX (613C to 618B): A last text of Gottschalk introduces his final indictment as an impenitent heretic. This is followed by the story of Hincmar's vain attempt to bring the obdurate monk to repentance during his last illness.

Hincmar's Closures

That this division of the material is indeed Hincmar's own seems clear: Each part closes in the same way, on a short explanation of intent. Thus, Part I concludes with the remark:

> Enough be said of those things. Yet many points remain regarding Gottschalk's blasphemies, against which — not as disputant, but as providing help to the simple — I will collect the following statements, like the previous ones, from the sayings of the Catholic fathers, lest we seem to the ignorant to fail to respond to all of Gottschalk's inanities....[42]

In contrast, Part II concludes on a general doxology that acts as a suitable ending to the book, and is not unlike the doxologies that abound in Gottschalk's own writings:

> Our imperfection will not be entirely detrimental to us if, being set on the way of God, we pay no attention to what is already done and we hasten to what is still to be done. For the One who enkindles the de-

sires of the imperfect strengthens them in some way, in view of perfection, through our Lord Jesus Christ, who with Him lives and reigns as God in the unity of the Holy Spirit, world without end. Amen.[43]

This doxology is followed by a new transition, which I read as introducing a lengthy appendix that must have been added later:

And since the same Gottschalk compiled several *schedulas* of his blasphemies, to all of which on account of our many occupations it has taken us a long time to respond, we have decided to write only of those which, as we have learnt, have brought scandal to some people.[44]

A similar transition, announcing a further disquisition against Gottschalk, ends section I and section XIV, where it introduces the next major division of the tractate. In the case of section XIV a doxology closes Part II, and the following transition introduces what I call the Appendices. That this tripartite division (two parts plus appendices, or, to simplify, three parts) corresponds to Hincmar's intent is, in light of these endings, virtually certain.

Notes

[1] This principle is formulated in the *Indiculus de gratia Dei et libero voluntatis arbitrio*, or *Capitula pseudo-caelestina*, an anti-Pelagian writing that is generally attributed to Prosper of Aquitaine. The principle is conveniently found in DS 246.

[2] *De divina praedestinatione* (PL 122, 356-440).

[3] *Liber de tribus questionibus*(PL 119, 621-648). Lupus added a compilation of texts from the tradition: *Collectaneum de tribus quaestionibus* (647-666).

[4] *De praedestinatione dei ad Carolum Calvum libri duo* (PL 121, 13-80).

[5] The position of the church of Lyon varied under its successive archbishops. Amalaire was very critical of Gottschalk, to whom he sent a letter of admonition (PL 96, 84-96). Under Agobard and his successor Remi (852-875), Hincmar could not count on any support from Lyon. His theology was first criticized in a sermon by Florus, who was undoubtedly the most able theologian of the city (PL 119, 95-102). The publication of John Scot's volume occasioned a sharp critique of Scot's theology in a document that was presumably composed by Florus, *Ecclesiae lugdunensis adver-*

sus Johannis Scoti erroneas definitiones liber (PL 119, 101-250). This was followed by another official document of the church of Lyon, *Liber de tribus epistolis* (PL 121, 985-1068), that is critical of Hincmar.

[6] *De praedestinatione contra Scotum* (PL 115, 1009-1376).

[7] *De tribus questionibus* (PL 119, 621-648), and *Collectaneum de tribus questionibus* (647-666).

[8] Text in Hincmar's *De Praedestinatione Dei* (PL 125, 63C-64A).

[9] The basic point of the synod of Valence is methodological: In speaking of grace and predestination one should avoid *novitates vocorum et praesumtivas garrulitates* ("novelties of words and presumptuous gargarisms"), and one should believe only what comes from the Church: *illud tantum firmissime tenendum esse credimus, quod ex maternis ecclesiae visceribus nos hausisse gaudemus* ("we believe that only that should be most firmly held which we rejoice to draw from the church's motherly bosom"). That is, one should follow the church fathers, "Cyprian, Hilary, Ambrose, Jerome, Augustine, and the others who rest in Catholic piety..." (canon 1, in Mansi, XV, 3).

[10] PL 125, 473D-618D.

[11] Some documents relating to the trinitarian question may have been lost; yet no reference to such texts is extent in the works of the main protagonists.

[12] René Rohrbacher, *Histoire universelle de l'église*, vol. VI [741 to 922], 9th ed., Montréjeau: Librairie Soubiron, 1903, p.407-425.

[13] *Gottschalk retrouvé* (*Revue Bénédictine,* 1931, p.304).

[14] "...une oeuvre où nul ne fut tenté de pénétrer... un fatras où bien peu d'historiens de la littérature théologique se sont risqués" (Emile Amann, *L'Epoque carolingienne,* vol. 6 of Fliche-Martin, *Histoire de l'Eglise,* Paris: Bloud et Gay, 1937, p. 337). Similar opinions are cited by Jean Jolivet, *Godescalc,* p. 82. The trinitarian controversy is omitted by Fernand Mourret (*Histoire générale de l'Eglise*, vol. 3: *L'Eglise et le monde barbare,* new edition, Paris, 1921), and by Eugen Ewig in Hubert Jedin's *History of the Church* (vol. III: *The Church in the Age of Feudalism,* New York: Seabury Press, 1980). It is summarized with pertinent observations by Schrörs, *Hinkmar,* p.150-161.

[15] Adolf Harnack, *History of Dogma,* vol. V, New York: Dover Publications, 1961, p. 302, n.1. Harnack adds: "The number of theological problems discussed at the date of this renaissance of theol-

ogy was very great.... But the questions were almost all exceedingly minute and subtle, like those suggested by clever children."

[16] Yet both the *Filioque* and the doctrines on predestination are studied: *The History of Doctrines,* Grand Rapids: Baker Book House, 1954, bk II, p. 30-34.

[17] *The Christian Tradition. A History of the Development of Doctrine.* Vol. II, *The Growth of Medieval Theology (600-1300),* Chicago: The University of Chicago Press, 1978, p. 59-61.

[18] With some other medieval writings one can draw information regarding the structure of the book from the manuscript tradition. In the case of Hincmar's *De una...,* however, there is no manuscript tradition. The text is found in only one manuscript: Bruxelles Gheyn 932 (Devisse, *Hincmar* III, p.1154). The text of this manuscript was printed by Jacques Sirmond (*Hincmari Archepiscopi Remensis Opera duos in tomos digesta....* Paris, 1645: Devisse, III, p.1157) and was reproduced in Migne.

[19] Devisse, *Hincmar,* I, p.166.

[20] PL 125, 480B.

[21] PL 125, 480C.

[22] Ambrose: PL 125, 480CD; Augustine: 481ABC.

[23] PL 125, 480D.

[24] PL 125, 481D.

[25] PL 125, 481D-482A.

[26] PL 125, 481D.

[27] PL 125, 482D.

[28] PL 125, 482D-483A.

[29] PL 125, 483A.

[30] PL 125, 483B.

[31] PL 125, 483C.

[32] *Hic famulus Hincmar Domini, sacra membra locavit*
   Dulcis Remigii, ductus amore pio... (PL 125, 1180D-1181B).

[33] Cited in PL 125, 1201, footnote a.

[34] PL 125, 1202.

[35] PL 125, 817-834.

[36] PL 125, 817B.

[37] PL 125, 822A.

[38] PL 125, 830C.

[39] PL 125, 832CD. There are also clear allusions to the predestinarian controversy. Such is Hincmar's summary of his position: "Those

who, by grace and following this grace by free will (*libero arbitrio*), will have persevered in the right faith and in good works, being foreseen and predestined to glory by God, will go to the eternal life prepared by God for the elect, that is, for those separated by grace from the mass of perdition of the whole humankind created in the sinning of Adam..." (824B). The precise point where Hincmar will be contradicted by the synod of Valence is the affirmation that salvation is by grace *and* by free will.

40 PL 125, 824B. In context, the identification of Eve with Adam relates to the universality of original sin and the "mass of perdition of the entire human race."

41 PL 125, 823BC.

42 PL 125, 510C.

43 PL 125, 579D-580A.

44 PL 125, 580A.

Chapter 5
DE UNA...: THE ARGUMENTS

The archbishop of Reims went to great pains building his case against Gottschalk. He made a considerable effort to gather the necessary documentation, undoubtedly with the help of the *scriptoria* of his metropolitan city.[1] While he often composed summaries of faith that were both accurate and eloquent, he was generally not comfortable with speculative considerations. However, devoted as he was to painstaking research in the manuscript collections of monasteries far and near, he was at his best in constructing an argument from the canonical tradition. For this purpose he gathered a dossier of suitable texts and tried to elicit their clear meaning. Since part of the problem lay in understanding the acts of council III of Constantinople, Hincmar obtained information, from an unknown source, regarding the exact meaning of several Greek words and expressions. The sum of the argument is that Gottschalk's condemnation rests on previous tradition: The new heretic has incurred anathemas that were formulated against the Arians. This argument is unfolded in the two main parts of *De una et non trina deitate*.

Part I: Refutation of Gottschalk's Thesis

The quotation to be refuted associates two passages from Gottschalk's *schedula*, taken from 476D and 478C.[2] The first accuses the critics of *trina deitas*, and Hincmar in the first place, of professing the twin heresies of Sabellianism and patripassianism. The second affirms that the absolute perfection of each Person of the Trinity (*ex trinitate persona*) requires that each have "its own perfect deity." This points is at the heart of Gottschalk's theology.

The archbishop's method is simple and clear.[3] Hincmar states what he has identified as the true doctrine. He attempts to overwhelm his adversary with quotations from councils, fathers, and theologians that support this doctrine. He concludes that both doctrine and tradition convince Gottschalk of heresy. A threefold pattern thus emerges: (1) statement of doctrine; (2) supporting tradition; (3) application to Gottschalk. What creates an apparent confusion in the text is the fact that, while the pattern — doctrine, tradition, application —

recurs several times in cyclic fashion, it is not always fully explicit, the statement of doctrine not being repeated in each cycle.

In a first cycle the traditional doctrine is posited (484A to 485C) and directly supported with suitable references to Scripture (484BC). There follow quotations from the fathers of the church with Hincmar's commentary. The texts are drawn from the works of Athanasius, Hilary, Gregory Nazianzen, Augustine, Ambrose, Jerome, Theophilus of Alexandria, Pope Leo, Gregory the Great, Prosper, Bede the Venerable (485C to 489A). These findings are then applied to Gottschalk in the vituperative style of the period: Gottschalk "blasphemes…"[4] "Either he does not understand what he says or he knowingly errs."[5]

A second cycle omits the statement of doctrine, and it refers to the councils of Nicaea I, Antioch, Sardica, Ephesus I, Chalcedon, the provincial councils of Africa, Constantinople II, Constantinople III, which is given considerable space (490A to 495B). Along with the councils Hincmar brings in supporting statements that relate to them, notably from Pope Agatho and Basileus Constantine IV in relation to the sixth council. The application to Gottschalk follows (495B-496A), with a vivid description of the wayward monk's fantastic offer to undergo a legal ordeal: Gottschalk is

> another Simon the Magician… agitated by a furious spirit, an excited heart, and raised eyes, lyingly promising to walk surrounded by miracles, asking that three vats be prepared, the first filled with boiling animal fat, the second with boiling oil, the third with ebullient pitch, and when, being plunged in each of them up to his neck, he exits unhurt, his assertion will be believed by all to be most true…[6]

The popular belief in the magic effect of legal ordeals was generally on the wane in the ninth century. It was dismissed by Hincmar as presumptuous and utterly ridiculous: "No one who is faithful and sober" can agree to such "deadly suggestions." One should rather oppose to him the "antidote" of true faith. In keeping with "the tenet of the Scriptures and the tradition of the ancients" one should refuse to debate with Gottschalk, as with all other heretics. One should simply sentence him, "as a spurious excrescence at the root of bitterness, to exile or to jail, isolated from the company of the faithful."[7] Such a treatment is supported by reference to Pope Leo, Ambrose, Augustine, Pope Agatho, Sophronius of Jerusalem, Proclos of Constantinople, Pope Gelasius, and the council of Chalcedon.[8]

A third cycle follows, that is focussed on the immediate occasion for the controversy, namely, the trinitarian formulas used in liturgical hymns. Again the true doctrine is not restated at the beginning, though it will be featured in the conclusion. The argument from tradition takes the form of praise to Benedict and Ambrose for their contributions to hymnody: Ambrose composed hymns, and Benedict prescribed their singing night and day in monasteries. Many hymns are "perfumed with the Catholic faith, contain pious prayers, and are of admirable style."[9] There is therefore no need for the one entitled *Sanctorum meritis inclyta gaudia*, "whose author," Hincmar says, "I have not yet been able to discover." This is "where *te trina deitas* is sung or rather blasphemed by some, by whom scandal is knowingly or unknowingly created in the church that is [already] attacked and hindered by many other troubles."[10] The application follows: The monks who sponsor such hymns should be treated as the council of Chalcedon and the African council of the two hundred and eighty bishops advised.[11] "Let them read the books of the orthodox at the times assigned to this by their rules, and they will find on the contrary that *trina deitas* is never believed…by any of the faithful."[12] At the end of the cycle Hincmar restates the true faith, with short quotations from Augustine, Athanasius, and Ambrose.

Three Conclusions

At this point the rhythm of Hincmar's writing changes. After the three cycles of argumentation that are shaped in the threefold pattern of doctrine, tradition, application, Hincmar formulates three long conclusions that allow him to express his main concerns as a monk, as an archbishop, and as a canonist. Thus he composes an exhortation to monks, *honorabiles fratres nostri monachi* (500A-505A), a statement on the authority of bishops and especially of metropolitans (505A-508C), and an invitation to all who wield authority to do their duty (508C-510C).

First conclusion: Monks are exhorted to choose the right way. Either they will share the blasphemies of Gottschalk and Ratramnus, who are themselves monks. Or else they will believe and sing in common with "the supreme heavenly Virtues, the spirits of the saints, and all the holy Catholic people."[13] Hincmar vehemently attacks Gottschalk, a miserable monk who is inspired "by an evil spirit." He accuses Ratramnus of falsifying the texts he has quoted from Hilary and Augustine.[14] The exhortation to the monks includes a warning to whoever would disturb the peace of the church[15] and an invitation to reflect on the eighth and ninth degrees of humility in chapter 7 of the Rule of St. Benedict. As Hincmar explains them, these degrees imply the duty to respect episcopal authority, especially in matters of pastoral care.

Second conclusion: If anyone does not follow these principles, the authority of metropolitans must intervene, in keeping with the canons of Antioch and the instructions of Pope Leo. In addition, the Benedictine Rule, chapter 2, prescribes severe punishment for recalcitrant monks: They should be whipped! Hincmar, who is familiar with the Rule, since he was a monk before he became a bishop, refers also to chapters 6 and 26. And he argues from Gregory, Augustine, and Leo that disciplining those who disturb the church's peace pertains to the duties of bishops.

Third conclusion: Hincmar addresses his colleagues, who have been made by God responsible for the church: "We too, pastors and doctors of the people committed to us, bishops and governors of the Church, rectors of monasteries who are called abbots...."[16] All such should enter into themselves (*ad nos redire debemus*) and examine their conscience to see if they have properly restrained heretics. Even Honorius, "pope of the great Rome," was anathematized after his death, because he had "decided against the faith."[17] The episcopal duty of vigilance is supported by reference to Augustine, Pope Felix, and Pope Celestine.

Part II: The Fallacy of Gottschalk's arguments

This section of *De una,*[18] the longest, contains Hincmar's main refutation of Gottschalk's arguments, that are ordered on a scale of descending importance. Being primarily a canonist Hincmar naturally begins with Gottschalk's reading of the sixth council, third of Constantinople. The interpretation of the conciliar text introduces linguistic considerations on the meaning of certain Greek expressions and their proper Latin rendering, along with a more fundamental grammatical discussion concerning the nature of singular (individual) and of plural (collective) terms. The historical and canonical debate and the grammatical discussion lead to reject Gottschalk's contention that each divine Person has "its own deity."

Hincmar argues by way of commenting on specific citations of his adversary that have been selected because he finds them particularly objectionable. The archbishop proceeds step by step to his own satisfaction, but in a circular manner that brings about a degree of reduplication, thus contributing to create an impression of obscurity and confusion. This method makes Hincmar's discourse excessively repetitive. Thus the archbishop discusses the sixth council twice (sections II, 510D-528B, and VI, 536C-538B). Gottschalk's central thesis regarding the formula, *trina deitas*, that was already heavily criticized in Part I, is brought up again twice for additional refutation (sections IV, 530B-532C, and V, 536C-538B). That deity is, in each Person, *singularis* (which I understand here to mean, distinguishable from deity in the other Persons), is also refuted twice (sections VII, 538B-540D, and IX, 550C-555D). In between, section III (528B-530A) examines the poetic use of Greek and Latin terms, that Gottschalk has adduced in his favor.

After his section IX Hincmar turns to more peripheral points. He disproves an argument from the analogy of baptism (X, 555D-560B). He examines the testimony of the poet Sedulius (XI, 560B-565C). He looks carefully at the conclusion of Gottschalk's *schedula*, which he divides in two sections (XII, 565C-572C, and XIII, 572D-578D). And he pays special attention to the last lines of Gottschalk's conclusion (XIV, 578D-580A).

Hincmar's ordering of his material alternates between his own reasoning concerning theology, interpretation, or grammar, and abundant extensive quotations from the fathers of the church. Confusing as this may be to the modern reader, it is significant of Hincmar's concern for tradition. In his eyes, contemporary discussion gains its proper value not from itself but from the fathers of the church, the councils, and generally the canonical literature it can muster in favor of its conclusions. The resulting mix is quite at variance with the equally variegated methods that are found in theological literature today. On the one hand, it underlines methodological differences between the ninth and the twentieth century. On the other, it is precisely what brought about the neglect of Hincmar's writings by most modern historians of theology, who cannot easily enter into his methodology.

Council III of Constantinople

Extensive consideration of the sixth ecumenical council was
prompted by Gottschalk's appeal to the acts of this council. Yet the
monk's reference to the Constantinople III was scant. The council,
he reported, condemned the Arians for worshipping "τριθεοτεία,
that is, three deities."[19] It also, at least in the edict of Emperor
Constantine IV, taught that "the trine deity is to be glorified." In
other words, in the language of the sixth council, trine deity did not
mean three deities. The argument was simple, and it was intended to
be most embarrassing to a canonist like Hincmar.

Yet the archbishop of Reims, respectful as he is, as a matter of principle, of the authority of councils, is not so easily impressed. For two
conditions need to be met for Gottschalk's argument to have any
value. First, the passage in question has to be included in the manuscripts and the canonical collections that Hincmar has gathered, for
he cannot simply trust Gottschalk's word that *trina deitas* was used
by Constantinople III. Second, if the text happens to be correctly
quoted, it is itself no more than a translation from the original Greek,
and one must ascertain that the translation is faithful. The archbishop,
in fact, was convinced that Gottschalk had falsified the conciliar acts
from which he quoted.

Unfortunately for Gottschalk, the passage he has quoted is not to
be found in the text of the sixth council. It comes from the emperor's
edict of promulgation of the synodal decisions.[20] But even then
Hincmar maintains that the authentic version of this edict does not
contain the words in question. As he explains the matter, he has sought
far and wide for relevant texts and he has borrowed a manuscript
from Peter, bishop of Arezzo. He has entrusted this manuscript to
the *scriptorium* of the monastery of Hautvillers, that was to make a
copy of it so that the original could be returned to its owner. Either
Gottschalk, in residence at Hautvillers, was himself the copyist, or he
had a chance to read the manuscript. In any case, Hincmar is persuaded that Gottschalk inserted the word, *trina* into a phrase that
actually said, *cooperante conglorificanda deitate*:

> This feminine adjective and movable word that has been placed here,
> *trina*, was, we believe, adulterated by Gottschalk when this book was

copied in the monastery of Hautvillers where he lived, from the authentic text that Peter, bishop of Arezzo, had sent me, as we read that
this has very often been done by other heretics.[21]

The archbishop, who has no proof to back up his accusation, tries
to establish a presumption that this must be the case. First, he extensively cites references to "Trinity in unity," and to "one deity" in the
emperor's edict and in the letters of Pope Agatho and of Sophronius
of Jerusalem that are included in the conciliar acts. The inference is
clear: The emperor could not have contradicted himself and spoken
of "trine deity" in the same edict. Second, Hincmar attempts to show
that Gottschalk's supporters are practitioners of the falsification of
texts. Ratramnus, he asserts, was guilty of the same dishonesty at
about the same time, when he compiled patristic texts from Hilary
and Augustine: "This compilation evidently shows up the compiler's
lie."[22] Hincmar reports that Ratramnus sent this work to the bishop
of Meaux, Hildegard. Some time later, as Hincmar was conversing
with others on the oneness of the deity, he referred to Augustine's
principle that what is said of God *ad se*, substantially, should be in
the singular, for it applies indifferently to the three Persons. One of
his collocutors, however, drew his attention to Ratramnus's compilation, in which it is stated that "truth [*veritas*] is an essential name"
and that Augustine spoke of *una et trina veritas* in *Against Five Heresies*.[23]

When he heard this, Hincmar borrowed a copy of Ratramnus's
compilation from King Charles's library. In it he read indeed: *Gratias
tibi, Deus; gratias tibi, vera et una trinitas, una et trina veritas, trina et
una unitas* ("Thanks to you, o God; thanks to you, true and one
Trinity, one and trine verity, trine and one unity"). Hincmar com-
ments: "As I read this I was most astonished, for I had never found
such words in this book, or ever in any book by any Catholic author,
and least of all in a book of the blessed Augustine."[24] Here again, the
archbishop understood *trina* to imply multiplicity. Hincmar then
searched in "many cities and monasteries" for the oldest manuscripts
of *Against Five Heresies*. Indeed, several copies contained the line
quoted by Ratramnus. But Hincmar was able to trace its source to an
interpolation in a manuscript of the king's library. Shortly thereafter,
at the synod of the five provinces, he brought the authentic texts,
along with the falsified version, to the bishops' and the king's atten-

tion. He clearly suspected Ratramnus of being responsible for the interpolation.

Undoubtedly, Hincmar went to considerable lengths in his investigation of Gottschalk's trinitarian doctrine. Yet his argumentation failed to establish that "Gottschalk changed the truth into lie as much as he could, substituting trine for three times (*ter*) or for Trinity in the edict of the sixth council."[25] In the first place, one cannot properly conclude to a falsification of the emperor's text by Gottschalk on the basis of a previous assumption that a text of Augustine has been altered by Ratramnus. In the second place, Hincmar himself admits, a few lines further down, that Ratramnus may have been working with a faulty translation from the Greek.[26]

The Meaning of *tritheoteia*

Gottschalk's fondness for the adjective *trinus* as a qualifier of the divine attributes brought him to a field that was not deeply familiar to him, the Greek language. There are, he argued at first, precedents for this use of *trinus*, notably among Latin poets. The theologian Prosper spoke of the "trine majesty" of God, the poet Prudentius of "trine piety," the poet Arator of God's "trine power." Equivalently, he continued, this is also found in Greek. The word τρισάγιον, designating the triple *sanctus* at the beginning of the anaphora or canon of the mass (at the end of the preface), is "properly, regularly, and catholicly" rendered, *trina sanctitas*, "trine holiness." Whence the word τριθεοτεία and the corresponding "most catholic" Latin formula, *trina deitas*, "trine deity."[27]

This is examined in Hincmar's section III. The archbishop dismisses the argument based on poetry: Prudentius and Arator were constrained to use theologically incorrect formulas by the metric rules they applied. And in any case Prudentius, like Prosper, employed correct formulations in other passages. Hincmar provides four instances where Prudentius poetically and correctly stated the oneness of the deity: "The nature of the three is one and the same;" "The essence of the three is one and the same;" "One equal deity is in the three persons;" "The one deity of the three is one essence."[28]

In regard to Greek, neither Hincmar nor Gottschalk was conversant with the language. Yet neither one hesitated to argue from it, the value of their argument depending largely on their sources of information. We cannot identify these sources. Hincmar, however, seems to be the better informed. He has no difficulty picking up Gottschalk's mistake: In a letter to Peter of Antioch, Quintanus Asculitanus translated τρισάγιον, not as "trine holy" (*trinum sanctum*), but as "thrice holy" (*ter sanctum*). Likewise, the hymn in the liturgy of St. Basil is not a "trine holy hymn;" it is "three times holy." The "three" of *trisagion* functions as an adverb, not as an adjective.

Returning in section VI to the argument from Greek, Hincmar abandons all reserve toward his adversary. Gottschalk, he writes, "wants to vomit what he has not digested"[29] when he translates τριθεοτεία as "trine deity." In so doing he opposes Marius Victorinus, "the teacher of St Jerome," Sophronius of Jerusalem, and Boethius. In reality, the affix τρι or τρισ, like *tri* in Latin, means *ter*, thrice, so that "the threefold repetition of the one God, when one says, Father and Son and Holy Spirit, does not place plurality in the essence; but one God is affirmed personally each time."[30] Trinity therefore means that "one total is made of three, like tri-unity, that is, thrice unity and not trine unity."

In contrast, the same affix signifies multiplication in words like triple, triangle, *triginta* (thirty), *trecenta* (three hundred), *triennium* (triennial), *trimus* (of a three year period, three years old), because in these cases repetition requires more time or more space. At any rate "it is not necessary for us Latins, who are ignorant of the Greek language, to labor for a long time"[31] over such questions, since one can read many orthodox books of authors who are well versed in the two languages. Gottschalk's argument is a lie.

The Role of Grammar

It is not enough, Gottschalk had written against Hincmar, to be a grammarian to avoid being a heretic. Hincmar retorts in section VIII that Gottschalk has been misled precisely by his inadequate knowledge of grammar. He has not noticed that words are of different kinds.

Tritheoteia, Gottschalk has argued, cannot be put in the plural, "as is known to all those who have only a mediocre knowledge of grammar."[32] As he wrote this, however, Gottschalk condemned himself. For he showed his own acquaintance with grammar to be superficial. He has not noticed a principle that is stated by the classical grammarian Donatus: There are nouns in the singular that have a plural meaning, especially words denoting people. Reversely, there are adjectives that imply plurality even when they remain in the singular, "such as *tertia* [third], *trina* [trine], *trima* [three years old], *trigama* [trigamous, married to three persons]."[33] Augustine places the word trinity in this category since it means a Trinity of Persons. One could indeed say, "the trine Trinity," for Trinity, like trine, is a singular word with a plural meaning. But one cannot say, with Gottschalk, "the trine deity," for the plural adjective would contradict the indivisibility of the noun. In this matter Gottschalk sins against grammar and logic no less than against the tradition of the fathers. Hincmar quotes extensively from Boethius, Ambrose, Athanasius, Augustine, Gregory, Hilary, Sophronius, Leo, and Prosper. Through them the Holy Spirit spoke. And it is only "the impure spirit that speaks through the most impure Gottschalk."[34]

In order to escape the grammatical difficulty Gottschalk gives deity a plural meaning. He boldly asserts that each divine Person has "its own deity and divinity;" and he claims to find confirmation of this in the incarnation, for, he argues, "by no means the whole Trinity but only the deity of the Son assumed humanity."[35] This, Hincmar responds in section IX, is "a lie more opaque than night, darker than darkness." Gottschalk is lost in a tunnel of obscurity and confusion where Hincmar cannot figure out what his words can possibly mean. Gottschalk's doctrine not only contradicts the teaching that only the Person of the Word is incarnate, rather than the deity that is common to the three Persons. In addition, it runs afoul of the council of Nicaea and the belief that the eternal Word is ὁμοούσιος with the Father. *Homoousia* implies that there is only one deity, common to the Father and the Son. Augustine is quoted to that effect, along with Leo, Athanasius, Ambrose, and Alcuin. And Hincmar states again his understanding of true trinitarian doctrine:

> In this way Catholics show that the heretic Gottschalk has lied, for it is not true that, as he says, in each Person in the holy Trinity there is present its own deity and divinity, but there are in the Trinity three Persons of one and the same substance, deity, and divinity, that is, of one nature or essence…. If each Person in the holy Trinity had its own special deity, the Trinity would not be one and inseparable, and there would be three gods.[36]

This is precisely the heart of the problem. Since divinity is common to the Three Persons in such a way that each is the totality of it, one may say that each Person owns its divinity, the only one there is, that is, the divinity of the Three. This is precisely what Gottschalk affirmed. Yet he evidently also believed that only the Word is incarnate, and that there are neither three Gods nor a divine quaternity or sexternity. Hincmar, however, considered this manner of speaking unorthodox; but it does not seem to me that he has been able to prove his case.

Arguments from Analogy

In the next three sections of his work (X-XII, 553D-578D) Hincmar rejects the validity of several analogies that have been adduced by Gottschalk. The monk has supported his trinitarian doctrine with an appeal to the structure of baptism, where three immersions make one trine baptism, not three baptisms,[37] and to the structure of faith, called *terna* or *trina* by poets Sedulius and Arator.[38] The archbishop is not impressed by these examples. He simply shows, as we have seen, that this is not the common manner of speaking: Arator allowed himself a poetic licence, constrained as he was by the metric rules of classical poetry.

Yet a more profound answer can be given in the case of Sedulius.[39] This answer comes from Hincmar's reflections on the nature of number. Gottschalk has contended that one is a Sabellian heretic unless one confesses with all catholics "*tritheotia*, trine deity, *trisagion*, trine holiness, the trine life, wisdom, glory, the trine fear, the trine love, the trine charity, the trine light, salvation, virtue, peace, clarity, the trine majesty, power, piety…"[40] In this, however, Hincmar objects, Gottschalk has confused the numerical adjectives, *ternus* and *trinus*.

There are in reality two kinds of numbers. In the first kind the repetition of one unit creates plurality and number. In the second kind "the repetition and plurality of units does not create a numbered diversity of numerous things."[41] The former are composite numbers, the latter simple numbers. The first kind implies plurality of objects, the second implies motion on the part of one object. "*Terna* is placed by those who study numbers, not among the composite but among the simple numbers, which have no other part than one single unit; and it does not come from the number by which we count three, but from the one [we use] when we say thrice (*ter*), having a collective signification." *Trinus* derives from *tres* and has a similarly plural meaning; *ternus*, from *ter*, has a singular collective meaning. Sedulius could properly speak of *terna fides*, because the faith that believes in the three Persons is one, not three. He intended to suggest that in God there is not plurality but motion, though not local motion, in the generation of the Son from the Father and in the procession of the Spirit from the Father and the Son.[42] The point is supported by an appeal to Augustine, Gregory, Boethius, and the venerable Bede, all of them students of numerology. Additional support is found in citations from Augustine, Sophronius, Ambrose, Alcuin, and Athanasius. In conclusion Hincmar oberves: "In order more completely to exhibit his stupidity, Gottschalk wanted to hide nothing; instead he has shown the full spirit of his stupidity."[43]

The Divine Attributes

Section XIII returns to the question of the divine attributes. Gottschalk qualifies all the attributes of God with the adjective, trine, as he does for deity and divinity. But is this compatible with a correct understanding of the attributes of God? The question is actually two-fold. One may ask if, the divine attributes being seen as, so to speak, radiations of the divine nature, it is proper to extend to them what has been affirmed of the divine nature. But one may also wonder if Gottschalk has not in reality reversed the process, and, taking the attributes of God as his chief paradigm, treated the divinity as an attribute of each Person.

According to Gottschalk, who, says the archbishop, is "stupid, impious, cruel, and an oppressor of God, in God light and peace are naturally one and personally trine."[44] That is, light and peace are at the same time attributes of the one divine nature and of each divine Person. To this, Hincmar opposes what he regards as the tradition: St Jerome, and the Roman liturgy of the vigil of Pentecost imply the opposite. When Paul says in Romans 1,20, that the "invisible things of God are seen in what has been made," he tells us to look at the sun: One cannot separate the sun, its radiance, and its heat. With the help of "these three inseparable things in the substance of one creature" we are to understand that, "just as in grammar the three are in the singular, so Father and Son and Holy Spirit, the creator of all that is, are one light and peace, not trine. For as God is Father, Son, and Holy Spirit, and yet not three Gods but only one, so the light is Father, Son, and Holy Spirit, and they are not three lights or a trine light, but one light is Father and Son and Holy Spirit."[45]

Hincmar's theological argument is well developed: Deity is a substantial, not a personal name. So are the attributes, since they inhere in the nature, essence, divinity, or deity of God, and not in the Persons. And yet the divinity is not to be confused with its attributes. The divine essence is so totally simple that "it can have in itself only what it itself is." Therefore in God "knowing is power, power is being and knowing."[46] All the divine attributes are one. Like the actions of God, they are performed by virtue of the one power that is inherent in the divine being, not by virtue of the relations that are distinctive of each Person. This is grounded in Augustine's understanding of divine nature as turned *ad se* while the Persons are *ad invicem*: "What is [in motion] toward something is not said substantially, but relatively and thus plurally."[47] It is also in keeping with Augustine's theology of appropriation. The actions of God in creation are performed by virtue of the divine power that inheres in the divine essence. Yet they may be appropriated, that is, attributed, to one Person insofar as they evoke a special relation with the creature that is particularly appropriate to what we know of this Person. And so the Father is called Creator, the Word and Son Redeemer, the Spirit Sustainer, although creation, healing power, and sustaining power are substantial attributes of the divine nature.

To this Augustinian theology Hincmar appends a curious grammatical argument. Discussing further the divine attributes of peace and of light, that were specifically mentioned by Gottschalk, the archbishop remarks that, in Latin, both *pax* and *lux* are words of three letters. Accordingly he finds in them a special symbolism. "When we say *pax*, *lux*, the three Persons in God are signified by the three letters, and since neither *pax* nor *lux* is put in the plural, the substance, that is, the deity of the one God, is indicated by the singular...."[48] Like Gottschalk, the archbishop of Reims believes that there are strict correspondences between knowing and being and between grammar and knowledge. This was an assumption of the culture of their time. That the argument requires the use of the specific grammar of Latin does not cause a problem to either of them, since the Carolingian view of language presupposes the fundamental identity of all grammars.[49] But the two opponents do not locate such correspondences in the same places.

The Conclusion

Citing the last sentence of Gottschalk's *schedula* in section XIV, the archbishop objects that the monk quotes Gregory the Great and then misapplies the quotation to himself. When Gregory wrote, "the one who is full of virtues applies the rule in spite of himself, the one who is void of virtues does not apply it even when constrained,"[50] he was thinking of the "spiritual person" of St. Paul (1 Cor 2,15), not of "the heretic Gottschalk." And, after citing Augustine, Hincmar concludes with a long reflection on virtue and the search for perfection. This ends with a doxology that we have already cited:

> Thanks be to God. Whatever we are, priests and those who have been placed in the government of the Church, who serve the Catholic faith in the body of Christ, from which Gottschalk has been expelled, we do not remain empty of virtues, for, as Augustine said, virtue is right or perfect reason.... Our imperfection will not be entirely detrimental to us if, being set in the way of God, we pay no attention to what is already done but we hasten to what is still to be done. For the One who enkindles the desires of the imperfect strengthens them in some way, in view of perfection, through Our Lord Jesus Christ, who with Him lives and reigns as God in the unity of the Holy Spirit. Amen.[51]

As Hincmar brings to a close his central refutation of Gottschalk's trinitarian doctrine, the heart of the question appears to be twofold. Linguistically it lies in opposite understandings of the word *trina*: Is the term divisive, the equivalent of triple, as Hincmar asserts? Or is it compatible with unity, designating the threefoldness of one nature, as Gottschalk maintains? Theologically the heart of the question lies in two areas. First, may the deity or divine essence be treated like an attribute of God, as Gottschalk does and Hincmar cannot do? Second, may one say with Gottschalk, and in spite of Hincmar, that each Person has its own divinity?

Notes

[1] Devisse, *Hincmar*, I, p. 233, 278.
[2] The numbers refer to the columns of Migne, PL 125.
[3] For an analysis of Hincmar's trinitarian theology that does not get involved in the intricacies of his conflict with Gottschalk, see Leo Ronald Davis, *Hincmar of Rheims as a Theologian of the Trinity* (*Traditio*, vol. XXVII, 1971, 455-468).

[4] PL 125, 489B.

[5] PL 125, 489D.

[6] PL 125, 495BC.

[7] PL 125, 495D.

[8] PL 125, 495D-498B.

[9] PL 125, 498C.

[10] PL 125, 498D.

[11] PL 125, 498D-499A.

[12] PL 125, 499C.

[13] PL 125, 500B.

[14] PL 125, 500BC.

[15] PL 125, 501C-503A.

[16] PL 125, 508C.

[17] PL 125, 508D.

[18] PL 125, 510D-580A.

[19] *Schedula*, PL 125, 478A.

[20] Mansi, XI, 710.

[21] PL 125, 512BC.

[22] PL 125, 512C.

[23] The *Adversus quinque haereses* (PL 42, 1099-1116) is not by Augustine, but neither Hincmar nor Ratramnus knew this. Hincmar did not notice that Alcuin had written something that comes close to Gottschalk's central thesis: "But these Three are truly three, and ineffably three, and essentially three, having their own qualities" (*Sed haec tria vere etiam tria sunt et ineffabiliter tria et essentialiter tria habentia proprietates suas*, as quoted by Gottschalk: Lambot, *Oeuvres*, p. 125).

[24] PL 125, 513AB.

[25] PL 125, 527BC.

[26] PL 125, 527D.

[27] PL 125, 528B.

[28] *…natura est una eademque trina; una eademque trium quoniam est essentia; una in personis par tribus est deitas; una trium deitas una est essentia…* (PL 125, 549CD).

[29] PL 125, 532B.

[30] PL 125, 552C.

[31] PL 125, 558A.

[32] PL 125, 540CD.

[33] PL 125, 540-541.

[34] PL 125, 548A.
[35] PL 125, 550D.
[36] PL 125, 553C.
[37] X, PL 125, 553D-560B.
[38] XI, PL 125, 560D-565C.
[39] XII, PL 125, 565C-572C.
[40] PL 125, 565CD.
[41] PL 125, 565D.
[42] PL 125, 567C.
[43] PL 125, 572C.
[44] PL 125, 573A.
[45] PL 125, 573D-574A.
[46] PL 125, 575A.
[47] PL 125, 576D.
[48] PL 125, 575B.
[49] On this point see Jolivet, *Godescalc*, 175-177.
[50] PL 125, 578D.
[51] PL 125, 579D-580A.

Chapter 6
DE UNA...: APPENDICES

For good measure the archbishop of Reims added two appendices to his already lengthy refutation of what he identified as Gottschalk's inanities in the area of trinitarian doctrine. The material from the monk's *schedula* that Hincmar had reproduced at the beginning of his rebuttal was exhausted at the end of section XIV of the *De una et non trina deitate*. There is every reason to believe that the refutation of Gottschalk's theology of the Trinity concluded originally at this point, marked as it is by a doxological affirmation in the style of Hincmar's conclusions:

> Our imperfection will not be completely detrimental to us if, being set in the way of God, we do not look back at past actions and we make haste to go on to those that remain. For he who willingly enkindles the desires of the imperfect strengthens them somehow toward perfection through our Lord Jesus Christ, who lives and reigns with him as God in the unity of the Holy Spirit, world without end. Amen.[1]

Yet other writings of Gottschalk's must have been brought to Hincmar's attention before his text was completely finalized. For now the archbishop introduces further discussion:

> And since Gottschalk has again compiled several *schedulas* of his blasphemies, to all of which our response has taken a long time on account of our many occupations, we have seen proper to write only of what, as we have learned, has scandalized certain readers.

In other words, Hincmar will now refute Gottschalk's ideas as these are formulated outside the *schedula*, in others of the monk's writings.[2] These appendices to *De una...* are in fact partially redundant. Yet they bring valuable additional considerations on three points of importance, namely, personhood in God, the difference between God's essential and personal names, and the nature of prayer to the divine Persons.

What Is a Divine "Person"?

The quotation from Gottschalk that opens section XV is simply called *Fragment III* by Lambot, who could not identify its source. But that its origin has not been ascertained does not diminish the importance of the text. This highly interesting passage clearly reveals Gottschalk's understanding of the term "person" as it has been traditionally used in trinitarian theology. The meaning of the term is contrasted with that of the word "nature" in the expression, "divine nature."

In the Trinity, the monk has written, nature "is nothing other than the general, common, and universal substance of all three."[3] This is faithful to Augustine's determination that nature designates what, in God, is *ad se*. It is, one might say, God in the selfhood of divine Being, or, in Gottschalk's vocabulary, the locus of "all Three's substantial generality, community, universality, unity." This common nature is designated by the expression, One God. To it prayer is commonly addressed. By contrast, a divine Person, Gottschalk has added, "is no other than the proper, special, and individual substance and essence of each" of the Three.[4]

This, however, is no longer Augustinian language. For the bishop of Hippo the Persons stand *ad invicem*, "toward" one another, and because of this they also are "in" one another. Thus, Augustine could not speak of one divine Person without presupposing and implying its relation to the other two. No divine Person could be said to be "in itself" or "for itself" (*en soi* or *pour soi*, to borrow the language of Jean-Paul Sartre), since each one of the Three is radically for and in the others. On the contrary, Gottschalk's perspective and his definition see each Person in itself, having special characteristics of its own that are not in the others. As he says, the difference between the one nature of God and the three Persons is "clearer than light: in the nature the substantial generality, community, universality, unity of all three are shown; in the Persons the individual specialty and property of each are declared." Gottschalk is then led to conclude: "By them [the Persons] the Trinity is manifested, and just as, above, there was the one nature, so in them is the trine deity."

Unfortunately for the student of Hincmar's trinitarian theology, the archbishop refutes this point by simply taking refuge behind Augustine without attempting to elaborate his own reflection on this central question of trinitarian theology. He quotes from two works of Augustine, *De trinitate*, bk VII, ch. 6,[5] and sermon 39 on the gospel of John.[6] In *De trinitate* the Persons or subsistences cannot be said to be "from" (*ex*) the essence, for they would then stand apart from and be other than the divine essence. In the passage that is criticized by Hincmar, however, Gottschalk did not say what Hincmar accused him of saying. He did not speak of the Persons being "from" (*ex*) the divine essence. He only referred to each of them as being "in" the Trinity (*unaquaeque persona in trinitate*). At this point, either Hincmar misread Gottschalk, or, being unable to find something objectionable in Gottschalk's expression he substituted "from the divine essence" for "in the Trinity." The archbishop was not above such a trick if he could gain a polemical advantage from it. Precisely, Augustine's quotation ended with the remark that "animal man" cannot understand these doctrines: This pointed to Gottschalk as not being a true monk, but *animalis homo*, an animal man, a beast.

Gottschalk's location of the Persons *in trinitate* evokes the expression he often used, *unus ex trinitate* ("one from the Trinity"). This formula was commonly found in perfectly orthodox contexts, especially in Greek theology. As Pope John II had agreed with Emperor Justinian in a letter addressed to the senate of Constantinople in 534, during the controversy against the Monophysites, Christ is "one from the holy Trinity" (*unus de sancta trinitate*[7]). The incarnation did not add a fourth person to the Trinity, for, as the fifth council (Constantinople II) taught in 553, Christ was no other than "the one divine Logos from the holy Trinity incarnate."[8] Hincmar, who was acquainted with the acts of this council,[9] must have realized that his argument against "from the Trinity" could be easily dismissed. The expression was in good standing. Gottschalk was following significant canonical and theological precedents that Hincmar, at this point, chose to ignore.

The citation from the *Tractatus in Johannem* comes from a polemic against Sabellianism. Augustine declared that number three, in the trinitarian context, suggests the relations and the Persons rather than the substance of God. It denotes "what is *ad invicem*, not what is *ad se*."[10] In consequence there is no question of mathematics in regard to God: "Number parts with number and is not caught by number." The archbishop's conclusion directly follows from this as he repeats a point that has been all along at the center of his polemic with Gottschalk: "With these words of St Augustine it is demonstrated

that Gottschalk speaks against the Catholic faith, when, as is his cus-
tom, he predicates [*praedicans*] a trine deity."[11] In other words, number — implied in the adjective, trine — cannot qualify the divine
nature, essence, or deity; it refers only to relations and Persons. One
cannot say, trine deity. Hincmar, however, does not try to discern the
reasons for the difference between Gottschalk, who frequently claims
to be faithful to the Augustinian heritage, and Augustine himself.
But this is not unexpected. The archbishop is more a canonist than a
theologian. Keeping the tradition requires faithfully repeating what
was said long ago by fathers and councils, as these interpreted and
applied the Scriptures. New ways are proper only when new circum-
stances call for new decisions. And these should not be taken by an
isolated theologian like Gottschalk, but by synodal meetings of bishops at their several levels.

Personal and Essential Names

The quotation that is adduced in section XVI comes from the same
unidentified text as that of section XV. There are, Gottschalk recog-
nizes with all who have reflected on trinitarian theology, both natural names and personal names of God. The natural names "are common to all three Persons equally, [they are] general."[12] This is standard doctrine, accepted by all schools of thought. But at this point
Gottschalk departs further from Augustine. For, he asserts paradoxi-
cally, the personal names "are by no means (*ullo modo*) relative names,
but rather essential or substantial, just like the natural names." Yet
each name belongs only to and designates one Person, being special
or proper to it.

That this passage was brought to Hincmar's attention is not surprising: It plainly contradicts Augustine. The archbishop had no difficulty gathering long quotations where Augustine and Boethius teach
the exact opposite. In Augustine's theology, what is said to be essential, substantial, or natural in God characterizes the divine essence,
substance, or nature, not the Persons. For additional ammunition
against his adversary the archbishop briefly cites Athanasius in the
same vein. The language of Augustine in this regard has in fact remained characteristic of Western theology as a whole. What is personal in God denotes one Person's relations to the other two. It is
true of one Person only. The Father is relative to the Son and vice
versa; and, in Augustine's perspective on the *Filioque*, the Spirit, pro-

ceeding from the Father and the Son as from one principle, is relative to both of them jointly.

A question that was of no interest to Hincmar may be raised today: Why Gottschalk's departure from Augustine at this point? The reason lies, I suspect, in that Gottschalk does not use the terms, personal and substantial, in the same sense as the bishop of Hippo. He gives a different meaning to "personal" when he declares that it is not a relative term. For him the adjective denotes what pertains to one Person, whether or not it also pertains to the others. Everything that is divine and therefore common to the three belongs to each of the Persons. Such is the case with deity, divine essence, being. The personal names may be called substantial since the whole divine substance pertains to and is present in or "under" (*sub-stantia*) each Person. This was not the usual language of the Latin fathers. Yet Gottschalk found support in etymology. The word *persona*, he believed, derives from *per se una*; it means "one by itself;" and this was taken by the monk to entail the negation, "not by relation to others."

Hincmar, however, had no difficulty uncovering the weakness of Gottschalk's argumentation. He located it in the etymological point and proceeded to a long digression on the derivation of *persona*. The correct origin of the word, he believed, is not from *per se una*. Boethius had the correct etymology: The noun *persona* comes from the verb *personando*. One is then faced with two possibilities. *Personando* can have a circumflex accent on the penultimate syllable, or an acute accent on the antepenultimate. In the first case, *personândo* is a form of the verb *personare*, meaning "to resound, to play music, to shout." In the second case, *persónando* "evidently derives from *sono*,"[13]the ablative case of the substantive *sonus*, sound.[14] It is still a verb, and it means something like "to strike a cord, to blow a trumpet, to make noise." The two meanings are very close. Admittedly these etymologies do not seem to be much more scientific than the first. They lead, however, to a different conclusion: "If he says that one speaks of Person in God because it is by itself [*per se una*] one deity or substance or anything of the kind, the Catholic faith does not accept it; for one and the same deity, which is the unity of the Trinity, is entire in each [Person] and in the three Persons together."[15]

Hincmar's refutation of his adversary, however, is overdone. The easy replacement of one etymology by another allows the archbishop to ignore the monk's substantive point. That the deity as such is entire in each Person, as Hincmar objects to Gottschalk, is certainly the heart of the trinitarian faith. But that was precisely at the center of Gottschalk's theology. It was in order to highlight the full divinity of each Person that the captive monk of Hautvillers qualified the deity as being personal to each of the Three. Given this emphasis there is no fundamental difficulty in calling the deity tri-personal, or simply trine. One may still argue that it is unwise to do so, or that it is not customary, or that it is pastorally imprudent because it can mislead the simple into a tritheistic understanding of God. Yet the substantial point that Gottschalk underlines would seem to be unimpeachable. If the divine Being is not divided among three Persons, but is whole and entire in each of the three, then there is reciprocity between Person and Being, Substance, or Nature. Each Person is the entire divine Being, and the divine Being is each Person equally and entirely. In Gottschalk's preferred language, what is then personal in God is also, in each Person, natural, essential, and substantial. In this case deity is properly called trine without any hint of tritheism.

Praying to the Persons

The next quotation from Gottschalk, at the start of section XVII, relates to the consequences of his doctrine for Christian prayer. It is a commonplace of the medieval reading of the bible that in the Latin rendering of creation (*Faciamus hominem…*, "Let us make the human in our image," in Gen 1, 26) the one God speaks in the plural. This is used to illustrate the point that even if the Old Testament does not speak explicitly of three divine Persons, it already puts plurality in the divine action.

What can be deduced from this exegesis regarding the difference between prayer to one Person and prayer to the three? Prayer to one, Gottschalk points out, is naturally couched in the singular: *Tibi Deo gratias*, "Thanks to thee, God."[16] But prayer to the three, or to one along with the other two, may well associate the singular and the plural: *Vobis Deo gratias*, where *vobis* is in the plural and *Deo* in the singular ("Thanks to you all, God"[17]). A more elaborate example is contained in this prayer to the Spirit:

> Come, blessed God, Lord Paraclete, — come, sent by the blessed God the Lord Paraclete, — in the name of the blessed God the Lord Paraclete: that all honor, praise, and glory be always and rightly to you all (*vobis*),

blessed God, Lord Paraclete, trine and one, and together to your blessed
Name and Numen (*vestroque simul benedicto nomini necnon et numini*).[18]

Not without reason Hincmar finds such a prayer totally confusing.
But his main objection is not to the obscurity or ambiguity of the
formulation, but to its untraditional character. Nearly eight columns
of Migne refute Gottschalk's way of trinitarian prayer. No other heretic, the archbishop asserts, has ever said anything like this. Hincmar
has no difficulty accumulating scriptural and patristic texts: God is
never addressed with a mixture of the plural and the singular. Examples are taken from the Psalms, Wisdom, John, Paul, Ambrose,
notably from his hymns, Augustine in numerous places and at length,
and Gregory the Great.

Nowhere, however, does Hincmar consider the doctrinal substance
of Gottschalk's contention. It is sufficient for him to show that the
fathers do not speak the monk's language. They speak, the archbishop
says, like David and Isaiah. When he substitutes his own form of
prayer to that of the seraphim that the great prophet heard, Gottschalk
betrays a diabolical pride. He pretends to a higher understanding of
"the divinity of the Persons of the Holy Trinity than the seraphim,
angelic powers in heaven, between whom and God no other spirits
mediate, and who even precede in dignity those heavenly armies that
are called Fullness of Knowledge."[19] Were Gottschalk right, these highest of angels "would sing with no understanding of what they say,"[20]
and King David, the prophet Isaiah, and the apostle Paul would also
be in the wrong!

"Unheard of Blasphemies"

Section XVIII continues to examine the previous quotation and
discusses how to address the divine Persons. More instances of what
Gottschalk considers to be proper trinitarian language are given.
Among them one finds the unusual statement, "Because it is from
the Trinity (*ex Trinitate*), each Person is by itself (*per se*) the Lord
God."[21] There is also an interesting paraphrase of the scriptural words,
"The Paraclete, whom the Father will send in my name" (John 14,26).
This can be rendered: "God has sent, sends, and will send God in the
name of God." Again, it is natural to invoke one divine Person in the
singular: "Thanks to Thee, God." But in order to show that the other
Persons are not forgotten one ought to add, "Thanks to You all, God,"

in which the plural, you, though it refers to the Persons, qualifies God in the singularity of deity. The one who so prays, Gottschalk concludes, is "truly Catholic and indeed a true Christian."[22]

This time Hincmar reacts with indignation. These are "hitherto unheard of blasphemies." The archbishop simply appeals to the tradition, that he illustrates with extensive quotations from Ambrose, notably in the doxologies of his hymns, from Athanasius, Augustine, and Alcuin. A comparison of Gottschalk's prayers with traditional forms of invocation shows them to be at variance with the Catholic manner of speech. This introduces the ultimate accusation that Gottschalk is insane:

> He has also written many other ridiculous things that we have found among his followers, to whom he gave them by fraud to be preserved, [and] that have seemed, not only to us but also to his accomplices, frivolous; and therefore we consider superfluous to insert them here, as they are the delirium of a maniac and old wives' tales (*aniles fabulas*)...[23]

Gottschalk's False Prophecy

A short transition to section XIX illustrates the monk's delirium. Several years back, Hincmar reports, Gottschalk confided to some of his friends that he had received a private revelation. According to this, Hincmar was to die a year and a half after this revelation, while usurping the power of authority like the Antichrist.[24] Gottschalk would then succeed him as archbishop of Reims, would be assassinated by poison seven years later, and would thus obtain the glory of martyrdom. One of those who heard of this revelation must have reported it to the archbishop. And his knowledge of Gottschalk's senseless hopes could hardly soften Hincmar's vindictiveness. In fact, as the archbishop duly notes, the prophecy proved to be false when the time passed for its announced fulfillment.

The final section of *De una et non trina deitate* is then introduced with a last citation, "one of his stupidities."[25] When he realized that the prophecy was not fulfilled, Gottschalk wrote to a young disciple of his. He expressed resignation to the will of God. But he also prayed for the archbishop's swift disappearance. Addressing "God who is present everywhere, the Giver of graces who eternally knows all things," the desperate monk is reported to have prayed:

Lord our God and master Jesus Christ, crucified only for the elect, who see that your enemies have made noise, and those who hate you have raised their head, because, six months after three years,[26] the robber and thief has not died, as was expected, I briefly but earnestly beg You all (*vobis*), Lord, our true and living God, one and also trine, to deal with him as soon as it pleases Thee. I do not wish for more, or sooner, or otherwise: When thou willst, may he be rightly plucked off, his life torn, the fornicator, blind, shameless, obstinate, unyielding heretic, the enemy of truth, the friend of falsehood.[27]

Hincmar has of course no difficulty quoting from Augustine, from pope Celestine in the *Indiculus de gratia Dei*, from Gregory the Great, and from Ambrose, to the effect that a true Christian, and indeed the whole church, pray for their enemies with love, not against them with hatred. Yet his la,guage in this conclusion is only slightly less vitriolic than that of Gotteschalk's prayer: "This pseudo-monk, in one way or another an adulterator of sincere faith and a blatant heretic, whose prayers neither charity recommends nor the Catholic faith accepts...."[28] Such prayers, Hincmar adds, are not answered. Whoever prays thus acts against the sacred canons and must be deprived of his ecclesiastical dignity if he has one. He "deserves to be cut off from ecclesial communion." There is more. According to the Rule of St Benedict, a monk who is "unrepentant, hard-hearted, and proud, or disobedient" should also be "subjected to flogging or corporal punishment, not only when he remains obstinate but even at the beginning of his sin." He should be separated from "the sane members of Christ," lest one sick sheep contaminate the whole flock.

In the last lines of this section, which must have been originally the last lines of Hincmar's treatise, the archbishop explains that he followed the Rule and applied the punishment in the first stage of the monk's heresies. He also reacted immediately to Gottschalk's false doctrine on the trine deity. Having already compiled his *De predestinatione contra Gottschalk* he was duly aware of the influence of the monk's false doctrine in the matter of predestination. The reader is thus made to understand Hincmar's concern and the haste of his reaction concerning *trina deitas*. The archbishop wished to avoid the kind of protracted controversy that was taking place in regard to predestination. This does not imply that Hincmar started writing immediately about the Trinity. Rather, he began looking up the matter,

and first of all by studying Augustine's *De Trinitate*, which is quoted
extensively in *De una*. At the same time he tried the pastoral approach, extending his solicitude to the monk, inviting him, personally, through others (*fratres meos*: the monks of the Hautvillers monastery[29]), and by frequent writings (*scripta*, which may include several letters to the monk), to renounce "his blasphemies against God."
But all this was of no avail. The soft approach led nowhere. *Saepe
commonui sed apud eum nihil profeci:*[30] "I warned him often, but I
had no success with him."

When Gottschalk Died

Within section XIX, but in what seems to be, as I have indicated,
an appendix composed after the death of the monk,[31] Hincmar narrates what happened after he was informed, presumably by the abbot
of Hautvillers, that Gottschalk, now very sick, was expected to die
soon. Ever a pastor even in the atmosphere of hostility that affected
his dealings with the recalcitrant monk, the archbishop made a last
attempt to bring Gottschalk to repentance and reconciliation.
Through the monks of Hautvillers he sent him an injunction, *schedula*,
that Gottschalk was expected to sign.

The injunction invited the monk to accept the true Catholic doctrine on predestination, grace, free will, and the Trinity. On
predestinaion Hincmar was careful not to condemn the teaching of
the bishops who had opposed him in the synods of Southern Francia
before the agreement of Tusey was reached. He only demanded the
confession that those who are saved are saved by God's gift, that Jesus
died for all, and that only the impenitent who refuse the gift are not
saved. On grace and free will Hincmar was now so diffident that he
did not specify a clear doctrine. He only indicated the sources of the
true doctrine, namely, the works of Augustine, Prosper, and "other
Catholic doctors" (*caeteri catholici doctores*). But the archbishop's cau-
tion, so different from his original assertiveness, made it impossible
to ascertain what exactly Gottschalk was to agree to. If it was the
doctrine contained in the works of Augustine that Hincmar used,
these included the spurious *Hypomnesticon*, a Pelagian production to
which Gottschalk could not reasonably subscribe. Regarding the Trinity the archbishop's injunction was more explicit:

This is the Catholic faith. We venerate one God in a Trinity of Persons, and a Trinity of Persons in the unity of deity, neither confusing the Persons like Sabellius so that they are not three, nor like Arius separating the substance so that it is trine. For the Person of the Father is other but not another thing, and the Person of the Son is other but not another thing, and the Person of the Spirit is other but not another thing. But of the Father and the Son and the Holy Spirit there is one divinity, equal glory, coeternal majesty. And in this holy and inseparable Trinity nothing is anterior or posterior, nothing is more or less, but all three Persons, Father and Son and Holy Spirit, are coeternal and equal, so that through all things, as has already been said, the Trinity of Persons is to be venerated in the unity of deity, and the unity of deity in the Trinity of Persons.[32]

As Hincmar reports it, Gottschalk got very angry when he was given cognisance of the document (*haec audiens in furorem versus*[33]). He continued to "blaspheme." But, after all, what could the monk do? What he had explained and defended regarding the Trinity was precisely, he believed, the true Catholic doctrine. That the archbishop did not see this was not entirely Gottschalk's fault, even if his language could have been misleading.

Admittedly, the proposed declaration can be regarded as mild. In it at least Hincmar attempted not to sound offensive or contemptuous. But the text was itself unclear on some points. It glossed over unsolved theological problems regarding predestination, and it entertained a surprising vagueness about the dialectics of divine grace and free will. On the question of the Trinity there was nothing in the deathbed *schedula* that Gottschalk could not have signed, except precisely the denial that deity may be called trine. Had he agreed to this, Gottschalk would have finally opted for the heresy that he had accused the archbishop of sharing with Sabellius. Given the choice of obeying the voice of metropolitan authority or adhering to what he perceived to be the true doctrine, there was no real option for the monk. He had to follow true doctrine.

Some time after the *schedula* was sent, Hincmar addressed a long letter to the monks of Hautvillers.[34] This contained his ultimate instructions concerning Gottschalk. The monks should try to persuade him to comply with the archbishop's conditions for reconciliation. In order to assuage their possible scruples about troubling the last hours of one of their own, Hincmar cited rules given by Leo,

Celestine, and Gregory concerning the impenitent who are about to die. Only those "sleep the slumber of peace," Hincmar explained, "who have not been severed from the unity and society of Christ and the church by heresies, schisms, or mortal crimes."[35] If at any time they have been severed from the communion, they can still be restored to it "through penance and the church's prayer." Should Gottschalk therefore repent his false doctrines he is to receive holy communion. But should he refuse to sign the archbishop's *schedula* he is not to be granted a Christian burial. He should be laid in a private ceremony outside the monastic cemetery.

To his very last moment, as Hincmar briefly narrates after citing his letter to the monks of Hautvillers, Gottschalk maintained "that he could not himself abandon his thought and doctrine (*sensum et doctrinam*) and receive the communion [offered] by authority."[36] Thus, Hincmar concludes, "he ended his unworthy life with a death worthy [of it] and he went to his own place." On these last words the *De una* comes to an end.

∗∗∗

This partly autobiographical section of *De una* related directly to the life and death of Gottschalk. But it remains an important source for our understanding of the two protagonists in the trinitarian quarrel. Each one remained as adamant as he had been since the beginning of the controversy.

Certainly the appendices of *De una* are not such as to convince the reader that the archbishop was a serene or even clearsighted theologian. Like much of what Hincmar wrote, the text is ponderous, pedestrian, repetitive. Here as elsewhere the archbishop of Reims remained a canonist who found himself forced by controversy to do theological research and to compose theological works. In regard to the trinitarian polemic the last part of *De una et non trina deitate* added no doctrinal point to what was contained in the previous sections of the text.

Notes

1 PL 125, 580A.

2 Hincmar does not explain the contexts of these quotations, and there is no guarantee that they all are entirely authentic. But their contents tally with Gottschalk's better attested texts.

3 PL 125, 580B.

4 The last word of the citation attempts to render the Latin, *singulorum*. The Latin form, which puts the adjective, singular, in the plural, has no exact parallel in English : *unaquaeque in Trinitate persona nihil sit aliud quam propria, specialis et individua singulorum substantia et essentia.*

5 PL 42, 944D-945A.

6 The text of PL 35, 1683 sends the reader to "sermon 36 of the gospel of John;" but the quotation is actually from *Tractatus XXXIX in Johannem*, n.3-4.

7 Emperor Justinian had asked…*utrum unus ex trinitate Christus et Deus noster dici possit: hoc est, una de tribus personis sanctae trinitatis sancta persona.* The pope then declared: *Probavimus in his catholicam imperatoris fidem…unum enim ex trinitate Christum esse, hoc est, unam de tribus sanctae trinitatis sanctam esse personam, sive subsistentiam, quam Graeci* ὑπόστασιν *dicunt in his exemplis evidenter ostendimus.* There follow citations from several Fathers of the Church (Joannes II: *Epistola ad senatores*, Mansi, VIII, 804).

8 See DS n.424, 427.

9 Devisse, *Hincmar*, III, p.1427; in spite of extensive reearch in the canonical collections, Devisse notes that he has been unable to ascertain which collection Hincmar used when he quoted from this council.

10 PL 125, 581A.

11 PL 125, 581AB. In this context *praedicans* does not mean, "to preach," but "to use a grammatical predicate," namely, trine as qualifying deity.

12 PL 125, 581B.

13 PL 125, 585D.

14 A long passage is quoted from Boethius, *Liber contra Euthychem et Nestorium* (PL 125, 584-585).

15 PL 125, 586B.

16 PL 125, 589A.

[17] The word, "all," is not in the Latin; I find it convenient to indicate that "you" is not singular but plural.

[18] PL 125, 589B.

[19] PL 125, 596D-597A.

[20] PL 125, 597A.

[21] PL 125, 597B.

[22] PL 125, 597D.

[23] PL 125, 613B

[24] ...*statim post tres semis annos suae revelationis* (PL 125, 613BC). There is no guarantee that the story is entirely true to facts. Hincmar had a vested interest in persuading his readers that Gottschalk was mentally deranged! The same point can be made about Hincmar's description of Gottschalk's death.

[25] PL 125, 613B.

[26] There is a discrepancy between the previous projection of "three half years," and *post triennium dimidio terminato anno* ("three years after the middle of the year" [or should it be, "three years and a half"?]). I cannot decide if the error is due to Hincmar, or if Gottschalk gave different projections at different times, or if the story was reported to the archbishop with varying embellishments.

[27] PL 125, 613CD.

[28] PL 125, 615B.

[29] The brothers in question are not other bishops but, Hincmar says, "our brothers (*fratribus nostris*) to whom we have entrusted his care" (PL 125, 615C). These are the monks of Hautvillers, whom Hincmar addresses also as "our brothers in the Hautvillers monastery" (*fratribus nostris in monasterio Altavillaris*: PL 125, 616C).

[30] PL 125, 615C.

[31] PL 125, 615C-618B.

[32] PL 125, 616AB.

[33] PL 125, 616C.

[34] PL 125, 616C-618B.

[35] PL 125, 617C.

[36] PL 125, 618B.

Chapter 7
LESSONS OF THE CONTROVERSY

The controversy of the ninth century on the Trinity was on the whole a minor episode in the history of Christian doctrine. It failed to stir up interest in its own time and it has attracted the attention of few historians or theologians. Yet it dealt with fundamental questions that deserved an answer. For both Hincmar and Gottschalk there were two related points. The first, which may be considered the heart of the matter, turned around the Christian doctrine of God: Was the liturgical formula that Hincmar outlawed faithful or unfaithful to the church's teaching that the one and only God is three Persons? The second followed, profoundly touching each of the two main disputants: Was either of them a heretic?

Each one denounced the other, Hincmar repeating that Gottschalk was an Arian, Gottschalk labelling Hincmar a Sabellian. In the eyes of posterity neither of them has been considered a heretic. Gottschalk was not an Arian or Hincmar a Sabellian. The problem that agitated them has been seen as one of speculation, not of faith. Yet the few who have looked at their positions have generally thought that Hincmar was right and Gottschalk mistaken. In this case, however, the fact remains that the disputed Latin hymn that occasioned the debate was used in the Catholic Church for the liturgical celebration of many martyrs until well into the twentieth century, before Latin was set aside as the language of corporate prayer. Moreover, the eucharistic hymn for the feast of Corpus Christi that is commonly attributed to Thomas Aquinas repeated without hesitation: *Te trina deitas unaque poscimus.*[1] The piety of the counterreformation gave prominence to this hymn in benedictions of the Blessed Sacrament. The growing ignorance of Latin may have blunted the sharp edges of the old discussion considerably. But it has not settled the question.

The Narrow Focus
The controversy between the archbishop and the monk was narrowly focused, most of the debate hinging around the conjunction of the words, *trina* and *deitas*. Yet both theologians were convinced that the Christian doctrine of God was at stake. I do not think they were entirely wrong. Yet the central issue did not lie where they saw

it. For Hincmar this issue was fidelity to the patristic and conciliar tradition. Gottschalk saw it more as a matter of trinitarian logic in the context of grammar. In either case the representation of the divine essence and the divine Persons was affected by the debate. When the controversy started, the Carolingians for more than half a century had been dealing sporadically with another problem of signification and representation, namely, with the question of holy pictures. In these conditions one may think that the emergence of problems relating to theological semantics was not accidental in a society that had been struggling for several generations with the religious signification of pictures.

Speaking and drawing, the use of words and that of paint, belong to different levels of human resources and skills. Yet both pertain to the area of communication. Their usage in a given society rests upon certain semiotic conventions. It makes sense when it applies to its object a grammar of representation that has been implicitly or explicitly agreed upon. Seen in this perspective the stakes were certainly higher than the unconcerned contemporaries of Hincmar and Gottschalk imagined, and even higher than the two heroes of the story knew. The doctrine of the *Caroline Books* about the images of the saints assigned a limit to Christian art that had long been left behind in the East. Can a Christian artist who paints an icon so suggest the mysteries of God that the image speaks not only to the intellect and the memory, as the Carolingians conceded, but also to the inmost dimension of the heart where the gift of faith inspires love and hope, as the iconodules of the Byzantine empire maintained?

Similar questions may be asked about the limits of language. What do human words describe when they designate the mystery of the Trinity, the unity of deity, the relations of the divine Persons, the origins of the Son and of the Spirit, the attributes of divine being? The Carolingians were prepared for this type of question by their enthusiasm about grammatical science, which they considered to be a science of reality and not only of signs. If words can express reality as it is, then it becomes of the utmost importance that the word be right. For if the word is not correct the reality that it describes as God can only be a false god, a demon, or an idol.

The early discussion of holy pictures in Francia had taken place before Hincmar and Gottschalk entered the scene. The doctrine of the synod of Francfort of 794 and of the *Libri Carolini* already belonged to what was recognized as the tradition. The problem recurred in their youth when, in 830, Claudius of Turin destroyed holy pictures in his diocese.[2] Yet neither of them had any basic reason to consider the problem of images as other than settled. Carolingian churches continued to be decorated, in several versions of the romanesque style,[3] with appropriate biblical and symbolic scenes that could be explained to children and to illiterate adults, and that served thereby a useful pedagogical purpose. The conflict that flared up in 859 between Pope Nicholas I and Patriarch Photius, which was chiefly started by the pope's indignation that a layman should have been elected patriarch, brought the question of pictures back to actuality in the guise of a general quarrel between Latins and Greeks. But when this happened the controversy on predestination was already in full swing, and the protagonists of our story were too busy to get involved in the question or to write, as others did, "against the Greeks."

Paradoxes

Readers of Carolingian literature have been puzzled by the controversy on the Trinity, by the heated language of its protagonists, and above all by the paradoxes that abound in the controversy. There is a first paradox in that to the modern mind the discussion was about so little that it would not matter very much who could have been right, Hincmar as he banned the phrase, *trina deitas*, as unorthodox, or Gottschalk as he defended its orthodoxy. The eagerness of the debaters stands in sharp contrast with the apparent superficiality of the problem. Given our general ignorance today of the nuances of Latin as a spoken language, we are not in a position to decide the linguistic aspect of the affair with certainty, even if some of us may be sufficiently conversant with Latin to lean one way or the other, and if there is evidence, as we have seen, that the crucial word *trinus* could be read in either sense, the one to which Hincmar objected or the one in which Gottschalk took it.

A second paradox is that the most profound theologian of the Carolingian period, Joannes Scotus, steered clear of the question raised by Hincmar. Reciprocally Joannes Scotus's investigations of the doctrine of God, which explicitly treated of the Trinity, were quietly ignored by both Hincmar and Gottschalk. The two of them were presumably too unfamiliar with the Greek world to appreciate the efforts of the learned Irishman to think Greek thoughts in the Latin language, and to gauge the extent of his success in doing so. Confined as they were within the limits of their Western world, Greek thoughts did not nurture their theology. Moreover, the philosophical and metaphysical mode of thinking, favored by Joannes Scotus, was too alien to the canonical mind of Hincmar and to the grammatical mind of Gottschalk to leave them with anything better than a general feeling of confusion before the speculative flights of Joannes Scotus. Indeed the Platonism of Eriugena would leave a profound imprint on later theology, both monastic and scholastic, through his translations of the works of Denys the Areopagite and his commentaries on some of these works. But it was powerless, in the kingdom of Charles the Bald, to break the contradictory trinitarian contentions of the archbishop of Reims and of the monk from Saxony.

There is a third paradox. Compared with modern ways of thought, the two protagonists were so similar. They naturally functioned within the same intellectual world; they shared the main ideas of the educated class, made predominantly of clergy, in the Carolingian kingdoms. Written language was still relatively rare; and as rarity made it precious, it was important to observe the rules for speaking and writing correct Latin. Hincmar and Gottschalk had received similar Benedictine monastic training, though in different institutions, and they had undoubtedly acquired a profound respect for the work done by copyists in the *scriptoria* of monasteries. They were awed by, and they tried to learn more about grammar as the chief adjunct science of theology. Both of them assumed that grammar holds the key to discourse, and thereby to intelligibility, and thereby to the meaning of reality and of the human encounter with reality in the experience of life.

In theology Gottschalk was more speculative than the archbishop. Yet both put great weight on the argument from precedent. They drew on their knowledge of the tradition in light of the documentation at hand, even if they emphasized different points. They mined the same authors for quotable passages. St Augustine was their main source and the early canonical collections their main resource. The heritage of the Latin fathers held their trust. In regard to Greek they both were handicapped by unfamiliarity with the language even while they argued about the meaning of some words and expressions. In this also they were typical of the growing estrangement between the respective theological approaches of East and West. For they shared the positions and prejudices of the Franks about the Greeks in general, the worship of icons, and the doctrine of the *Filioque* in particular.

Moreover, the two adversaries did not disagree on the structure of the church. Gottschalk denied the archbishop's doctrine, not his authority. And the archbishop, even when he was treating Gottschalk harshly, remembered that he had himself been a monk, and wished to remain within the bounds of customs and practices foreseen in the Rule of St Benedict.

Metropolitan authority

At the higher levels of church authority the Franks had been for about one century the main political supporters of the pope in Rome against sporadic incursions by aggressive Lombards and the occasionally heavy pressure of the weakening Byzantine empire. Yet they generally disagreed with the popes of the recent past, notably with Gregory II and Gregory III, in regard to the place of icons in Christian piety and doctrine. Rather than follow recent or contemporary bishops of Rome they adopted the opinions of a prestigious pope of the more remote past, Gregory the Great, and the doctrine contained in his letters to Serenus.

There also was a second fault of dissent between Reims and Rome. Hincmar was suspicious of the Roman claim to supreme authority over against the traditional authority of archbishops or metropolitans. The church that he lived in and worked for was not only local at the level of his diocese, and universal at that of the Roman primacy. It was above all metropolitan or provincial, the ecclesiastical province acting as a kind of middle judicatory between local and universal authorities, sharing to some degree the responsibility of both. This was in keeping with the ecclesial reforms of Charlemagne, who preferred to deal directly with a small number of metropolitans wielding real authority over bishops than with a multitude of bishops. Located in the middle level of the episcopal hierarchy, Hincmar was eager to maintain his provincial power over suffragan bishops who wished to assert their independence, and also to protect it from badly informed, incompetent, or excessive interventions of the bishop of Rome. Several times Hincmar took it on himself as metropolitan to correct the behavior of bishops in his province. Rothade had been bishop of Soissons since 832. Over the years Hincmar found him lax in his episcopal duties, notably in his attendance to synods, and he vainly urged him to a more exact application of the canons. In 861 he persuaded a provincial synod to excommunicate Rothade, who was deposed in 862 at the synod of Pîtres. But the bishop of Soissons appealed to the pope, travelled to Rome, and was restored to his see by Nicholas I in 865.

It was largely, though not only, because of diverging conceptions of episcopal and metropolitan authority that Hincmar had a fight with his own nephew, Hincmar of Laon.[4] But the young bishop of Laon held another view of metropolitan authority than the archbishop. Relying on the *False Decretals* and promoting their ecclesiology, the younger Hincmar wanted to free the bishops from excessive royal and metropolitan authority. But he had no political common sense. When he espoused the cause of the king's rebellious son Carloman, Hincmar of Laon made a powerful enemy of Charles the Bald. Carloman had been offered to a monastery and had been made a deacon at the age of twelve, but his ambitions were political and military. After some successes roaming the countryside of Burgundy at the head of a private army, he failed. At the assembly of Attigny, that he was forced to attend in May 870, Carloman was excommunicated. Arrested and confined to a residence at Senlis, he was soon blinded by the king's agents as a final measure to prevent further revolts.

Meanwhile, accused by his uncle of rebellion against the superior authority of his metropolitan, Hincmar of Laon was deposed by the synod of Douzy in April-May 871. With Charles the Bald the bishop of Laon passed through periods of friendship and trust that were succeeded by periods of royal aggravation and anger, until the king finally lost patience with the supporters of Carloman's rebellion. After his deposition Hincmar of Laon was also imprisoned. Eventually he shared the awesome fate of Carloman, being blinded by order of Count Boso, King Charles's brother-on-law, under whose care he was imprisoned, and who feared Hincmar's intrigues during the king's visit to Northern Italy.[5] Hincmar of Laon was nonetheless authorized to celebrate mass by the fifth session of the synod of Troyes of 878, that met in the presence of Pope John VIII.[6] Although he was granted a pension on the revenues of his former diocese the blind and sick bishop was not restored to the see of Laon. He led a diminished existence until he died a few months later. He had lost a battle that he had no chance to win. But the archbishop had gained little more in the process than the satisfaction of upholding the canons, and a lot of bruised feelings.

Hincmar of Reims himself never travelled to Rome. He corresponded with the successive popes, and he rebuked them on occasion. His relations with Nicholas I were particularly strained. Their theories on the church's structure and hierarchy were mutually incompatible. And both were excessively authoritarian in their style of government. Nicholas, who was bold enough to try to dominate the patriarchal see of Constantinople, could not be too impressed by the claims of a metropolitan on the borders of Francia and Lotharingia. But the archbishop did not hesitate to oppose the pope, especially when papal intervention in local questions of which the bishop of Rome could have no personal knowledge had a deleterious effect for the church and its people. This was the case in regard to Norman raids along the great rivers of the Frankish empire. Though Pope Nicholas and the archbishop occasionally relied on each other, they were never friends. Yet even if from time to time the pope found the archbishop of Reims across his path, he generally obtained Hincmar's support in specific cases, except when King Charles the Bald's major interests were at stake. Hincmar usually, though not always and not systematically, took the king's side.

Gottschalk did not express himself on the structure of the church. He may have made a pilgrimage to Rome before his troubles began, when he was traveling in Italy, but this might denote no more than a devotion to the apostles Peter and Paul. It may be significant that he did not appeal to the bishop of Rome against the archbishops of Mainz or of Reims, even when his position on predestination had the clear support of the bishops of central and southern Francia. Whatever appeals he did make were addressed to his peers, the theologians, not to bishops.

There were indeed remarkable personal differences between Hincmar and Gottschalk. Though equally stubborn, they were of totally opposite temperaments, and their mentality had been shaped by quite different experiences. On the one hand the archbishop of Reims had been unalterably successful in his career, first as a monk at St Denys, then as a courtier attending to spiritual needs at the court of Louis the Pious and of Charles the Bald, and finally as archbishop in the main see of Northern Francia. Gottschalk on the other hand could be considered a failure. He was, in a sense, the victim of an oppressive system. Offered by his parents to the monastery of Fulda as a boy, he was forced as a young man to remain in the monastic life against his better judgement, by what would later be considered abuses of authority on the part of the abbot, Raban Maurus himself, and of the king. Years later during the predestinarian controversy he was publicly humiliated, flogged, forced to destroy his writings, and then deprived of much of his freedom for the rest of his life, and all this because of his theological conceptions and of the inability of his adversary to persuade him of error. Their outlooks on the desirability and nature of the monastic life and commitment were totally different, as was also the general orientation of their careers.

Yet Hincmar was as much of a driven man as Gottschalk. But the two were not following the same vision. Hincmar was above all a servant of the church, its structure, its laws, its justice, all of them of course being at the service of the work of Christ the Savior in this sinful world. Given the majesty of law, charity must take a back seat in the proper ordering of society, whether in kingdom or in church. The pattern of orthodoxy having been set by the early councils and fathers, theological innovation is to be discouraged, and nothing is secure unless it is done according to the decisions of contemporary authority, especially that of metropolitans and of provincial synods. Gottschalk's vision was at odds with this. It was focused on the contemplative dimension of faith, a contemplation that is served by both poetic and theological expression. The councils are important, but they should be interpreted in light of the theological tradition, especially that of St Augustine.

The Problem of Representation

These radical differences between Hincmar and Gottschalk suggest why they further embittered their already sharp quarrel about predestination with an additional polemic about the Trinity. I will approach this theme with reflections on two aspects of the polemic that are particularly intriguing: the ties of the question of *trina deitas* with the problem of icons; and the contrast between the disagreement between Hincmar and Gottschalk on *trina deitas* and their agreement on the *Filioque*.

Both Hincmar and Gottschalk inherited a theology of religious art from their Carolingian predecessors. Now the question whether pictures can be holy, as the Greeks affirmed at Nicaea II and as the Franks denied in the *Libri Carolini*, is fundamentally a question of communication: What can the art of painting communicate? The question may be made more precise. In both East and West the painters stood in the artistic tradition of the Roman empire that is still visible today in Pompei and other archeological sites, but the Christian artists drew their subject matter from the treasury of the church's tradition. Painters illustrated the prophetic preparation of the church in the Old Testament, its origin in the incarnation and in the events of Christ's life, death, and rising, its history in the lives of the saints. This could not be done by simply conveying to the eyes what is stated in the letter of Scripture or manifest in the events of history. It required the opening of painter and painting to the spiritual world to which believers have access by faith.

In order to facilitate entrance into this spiritual dimension religious painters abide by certain stylistic conventions. These conventions were made in light of the christological dogmas endorsed by conciliar decisions. This was entirely deliberate in the East, where liturgical painters were bound to follow the instructions of the Quinisext council of 691-692. Rule n.82 enjoined church decorators to depict the humanity of Christ rather than the symbol of the Lamb.[7] Both ways of pointing to Christ — the realistic and the symbolic — had been common in the early paintings and sculptures of the catacombs. But at the end of the seventh century, after the crisis of monotheletism, the focus on the humanity of Christ helped to promote the christology of Chalcedon, as the minds of worshippers were opened in faith to the divinity of Christ and to the heavenly world. After the iconoclastic crisis, the second council of Nicaea, followed by later synods, confirmed and expanded the principle of the Quinisext council. Carefully promoted by bishops and synods, icon-drawing grew in depth, interconnected as it was with ascetic and mystical life in monasteries of the Basilian tradition. Icons became ways of perceiving the divine presence through the redeeming and deifying power of Christ in himself and in his saints.

These principles were also applied in the West, though not so consciously and to a more limited extent. Many of the motifs of Western church art were inspired by Eastern miniatures. Yet the artists and craftsmen who worked in Gaul or in Spain in the romanesque style that was familiar to the Carolingians were generally not aware of following the ecclesiastical canons of the East, which had no parallel in the Western synods. Likewise, miniature painters in Ireland and, in the wake of St Colomban, in Irish monasteries on the continent, were not consciously following Greek canons. At the crossroads of a multitude of influences, they created the style of Christian represen- tation that was made famous by the *Book of Kells*, the illuminations of which were crafted shortly before the time of Hincmar's life, in the last quarter of the eighth century or the beginning of the ninth.[8]

That theology can be non-verbal was nowhere, at the time, a point of contention. But a further question was not settled in the same way by the Greeks and by the Franks: What kind of theology is the non- verbal system of communication that is traced by lines and paints on a two-dimensional surface according to accepted canons of ecclesial style? There is no essential divergence in the technique of representa- tion and in the work of artists between the Byzantine art of icon drawing, the celtic art of mixing the human figure with convoluted geometric designs, and the Carolingian art of painting. The differ- ence comes from the dimension that on-lookers and visitors add to the work. To the Greeks icons convey a contemplative theology that is profoundly related to life in Christ and the Spirit, and which, pro- ceeding from grace to grace, leads the faithful soul along the way of deification. Icons are, scholastic theologians could have said, sacra- mental. To the Franks, however, church paintings act only as media of instruction and means of decoration. Proceeding from intellect to intellect, their images convey a catechesis and a didactic theology. Pictures and statues are not sacramental.

Rome, at the time, kept a foot in each camp. Roman bishops and synods approved and supported the Eastern understanding of icons against the restrictive sacramentalism of the iconoclasts. Official Ro- man policy did not stay within the minimalist positions of Gregory the Great. At the level of theory it was in agreement with Greek thought. Yet the Greek view had not shaped the Latin liturgy or touched Latin forms of devotion. Roman modes of piety remained nearer to those of the Franks than to those of the Greeks, with the major difference that while the Franks attacked the Greeks in the name of Western customs, Rome, then more flexible in non-essential matters than it became later, found no ground to oppose the piety of the iconodules and the principles on which it was based.

The Scope of Symbols

When, attentive to canonical orthodoxy in his diocese, Hincmar banned the singing of *trina deitas*, the question raised about the meaning of *trinus* hid another, logically antecedent, question: What level of reality do symbols reach? Directly, the decision affected one linguistic symbol, the word *trinus* as a qualifier of deity. Indirectly, it raised a question about the entire range of language: Are words to be taken in their strict denotation, or can they be understood according to the indefinite aura of their connotations? Still more indirectly the ban raised a similar question about the broader semiotic field. Whether pictorial or linguistic, symbols are intended by their creator — here, a speaker or a painter — to convey something, a notion, an idea, an image, a feeling, possibly a sensation. They are in turn used by their perceiver, as auditor or as spectator, in a constructive synthesis in which something emerges in the perceiver's consciousness that more or less corresponds to the creator's intention. The reader of the symbol reconstructs a notion, an idea, an image, a feeling, or possibly a sensation.

This is precisely where a connection is manifest between the theological debate on holy picture and the quarrel over trinitarian language. Hincmar's question about words was germane to what had been asked in the *Caroline Books* and by Claudius of Turin about pictures. Yet neither Hincmar nor Gottschalk or any of their contemporaries seem to have perceived this link. The *Caroline Books* had in fact connected icons and language in that they paid attention to both the Greek doctrine about icons and the Greek denial of the *Filioque*. They had criticized the Greeks, at the cost of also opposing the mediating Roman position on icons and Pope Leo III's compromise in regard to the procession of the Holy Spirit, accepting the doctrine but refusing to make it a matter of faith by putting it into the creed.

The temporal proximity between the emergence of an official Carolingian position on holy pictures and the start of the trinitarian controversy highlights their theoretical closeness. Both movements were constrained by the theoretical limits of symbolic communication. Hence a puzzling aspect of the controversy. Neither Hincmar nor Gottschalk expressed himself on the downgrading of icons in the empire of the Franks. On the one hand Hincmar could have drawn support from it for his concern that language be not abused. He

could have argued that words, and notably *trinus*, remain, like
Carolingian pictures, exterior to the reality they denote. On the other
hand, had Gottschalk pushed his logic further, he could have ascribed to pictorial representation the spiritual dimension by which
words refer to the divine being. Words can be verbal icons, giving
access to the reality of *deitas*. The *trinus* of a hymn does not simply
state that the Trinity of Persons is a Trinity of the deity. It also places
the singer in a worshipping attitude before the mystery of the three
Persons who are one.

Poetry and Icons

The poetic use of language, which was familiar to both disputants
and was practiced by Gottschalk with great delicacy, is not dissimilar
from the iconic use of paint. Icons point to the spiritual world that
they depict. When Gottschalk adduced poetic texts in favor of his
position he pointed to precedents to his use of the expression *trina
deitas*. Hincmar responded by quibbling about the literal meaning of
the adjective and by dismissing its use by Arator as poetic licence. In
their exchange, however, both adversaries missed the central thrust
by which poetry reaches beyond the obvious as it opens a gate to-
wards hidden, mysterious dimensions of existence and experience.
Although he was a sensitive if not an abundant poet, Gottschalk did
not respond at the level where poetry could have truly helped him.
Being a more delicate poet than Hincmar he would have been in a
better position to see that poetry, through its different discourse, leads
to another kind of insight than is obtained from the merely correct
formulation of doctrine. Poetry does not assume that truth is
adaequatio verbi et rei, as when reality is taken to be the object of
sensory experience. It locates the power of words in their evocative
capacity rather than in their designation of objects. It treats the se-
mantic dimension of language according to its allegorical connotations, being often assisted in this by the sounds of phonemes and the
rhythmic cadences of accents and verses. In this process poetry re-
veals a deeper *adaequatio verbi et rei*, in which *verbum* is discourse
rather than word, and *res*, hidden to the senses, is inwardly unveiled
and revealed. Behind the dimension of poetic language there lies the
poetic dimension of language.[9] Yet neither this dimension of language nor poetic language as such appears in Gottschalk's defense of
the hymn that Hincmar has condemned. This line of argumentation

could not have been used without implicitly undermining the Carolingian consensus about holy pictures. Whether he thought of this is even doubtful: Gottschalk was very much, like Hincmar, a child of his place and time.

As for Hincmar, he may well be excused. For he was not as good a poet. As an ecclesiastical scholar he was a canonist rather than a theologian. As a canonist he was more a compiler of legal texts than an interpreter of law. Except in several summaries of doctrine that are not only exact but also truly eloquent and spiritually profound, his use of words did not normally soar above the pedestrian level of their literal sense, popular or technical. When the archbishop heard the word *trinus*, whether in ordinary language or in hymnody, he spontaneously counted "one, two, three." Counting, however, does not lead to the Trinity but only to the idolatric pretense of three gods. Hincmar therefore affirmed *una deitas* only. When Gottschalk heard the same word in the liturgical context of a traditional hymn he did not count, but the eyes of his soul caught a glimpse of the deity that was revealed through Christ as three Persons, *trina deitas*. And because, in spite of what Hincmar was saying of him, he believed in one God, he specified, *una et trina deitas*.

Trina deitas and the *Filioque*

The archbishop of Reims and his opponent disagreed about the nature of the divine unity. Yet they both professed Augustine's doctrine, as endorsed by the *Caroline Books* and the Frankish council of Francfort, that the Spirit proceeds from the Father and from the Son as from one principle. Unlike Ratramnus, Aeneas of Paris, or Jonas of Orléans, neither one argued the matter in a polemical work against the Greeks. Yet both professed the *Filioque* when they had an occasion to do so. Hincmar included it in the trinitarian creeds and doxologies that are dispersed in his writings. The archbishop was a man of the Carolingian establishment, in which the double procession of the Spirit had been an official doctrine since Charlemagne. In fact he himself saw a close tie between the *Filioque* and his own understanding of *unus* and *trinus*.

This is manifest in Hincmar's explanation of his poem, *Ferculum Salomonis*. This explanation must have been written after the start of the trinitarian controversy, for in it Hincmar carefully states why unity qualifies deity and Trinity qualifies the Persons:

...in all things the unity of deity is in the Trinity of Person and the Trinity of Persons is in the unity of deity, because from the Father alone, that is, from the substance of the Father, the equal and consubstantial Son is generated, not created, and from the Father and at the same time from the Son (*ex Patre simul ac Filio*) the coequal and consubstantial Holy Spirit equally proceeds.[10]

Thus Hincmar saw the reason for the non-equivalence of trinity and deity in the origin of the Son "from the Father alone," and of the Spirit "from the Father and from the Son."

In these conditions it would seem that Gottschalk could have logically taken his distance from the *Filioque*. The Saxon monk was indeed a free person in theology no less than in the practice of the monastic life. Anxious to follow the doctrinal tradition, he was not afraid to lecture his peers and his superiors as to the tenure of authentic teaching. He had given deep thought to the divine Persons and had identified the divine threefoldness as affecting the very deity of God. In so doing he had used language that derived from an original understanding of the *homoousios* of Nicaea I and the *homoousia* of Constantinople III. Since the attributes of God share the *homoousia* of the Persons, so do they share their threeness. Each is one and trine along with the deity. The divine *ousia* being originally the Father's and the Father himself, it belongs to the Word and it is the Word by virtue of divine begetting, and it belongs to the Spirit and is the Spirit by virtue of divine procession. Like the *ousia* each attribute is total and perfect as the Father's attribute. It gains nothing from being given to the Son and to the Spirit, other than the very sharing of it and the three Persons' communion in it. Likewise, what the Father does in the procession of the Spirit is perfect and total in itself. This is the gift of deity and of all that belongs to deity, namely, being, oneness, goodness, beauty, almightiness, infinity, and an infinity of attributes. The Gift needs no complement or supplement from the Word. In the perspective of Gottschalk's trinitarian theology the *Filioque* appears therefore to be superfluous. Yet this is not what Gottschalk ever said. The captive monk of Hautvillers maintained the *Filioque*.

Why, then, did he do so? What could have stopped him from taking a new look at the procession of the Spirit? Could he not have seen the third Person in the light of the assimilation of divine attributes and divine *ousia* that characterized his vision of God? Four difficulties must have stood in the way of such a move. Firstly, Gottschalk never took seriously the arguments of his adversary. Secondly, he did not read Greek well enough to gain a personal acquaintance with the theology of the Greek fathers and with the Greek acts of the great councils. Thirdly, he fully intended to be faithful to Augustine against what he identified as the infidelities of the archbishop of Reims; and it was Augustine who had unequivocally taught the double procession of the Holy Spirit. Fourthly, the only theologian who broke the Carolingian consensus against the *Filioque*, Joannes Scotus, had himself violently attacked Gottschalk's predestinarian theology and denounced the monk of Orbais as a confused and foolish heretic: Gottschalk could have felt no incentive to agree with the Irishman.

Some Lessons of the Story

It is always somewhat hazardous to draw lessons for the present from a long forgotten controversy. Such lessons in any case do not bear on the problem that agitated Hincmar: Is *trina deitas* orthodox? It would serve no useful purpose to revive Gottschalk's understanding of deity, although I see no basic reason why his key to trinitarian theology could not today be an acceptable and effective alternative in the Christian approach to the divine mystery. But the lessons of the story lie elsewhere.

Developments of trinitarian thought among the scholastics and in the later medieval councils turned around other points. The Roman tradition of Leo III was abandoned when Pope Benedict VIII (1012-1024) accepted the insertion of the *Filioque* in the Latin creed at the coronation of Emperor Henry II, in Rome, on 2 February 1014. What had been a *theologoumenon*, a respectable theological conclusion, and a pious teaching, began to function as an undefined dogma of the Western church, the previous Roman creed of Pelagius I progressively falling into oblivion. In 1215 the *Filioque* was endorsed by the Fourth Council of the Lateran.[11] Meanwhile, the investigation of trinitarian doctrine explored other areas: the balance of similarity and dissimilarity between the Creator and creatures, as suggested by the same Lateran Council,[12] the different definitions of personhood by Richard of St Victor and Thomas Aquinas,[13] the nature of relations in scholastic theology, the connection of personhood with "op-

position of relation" at the council of Florence[14] (1442). The accep-
tance of the *Filioque* by Basileus Michael Paleologos at the second
council of Lyon[15] (1274) was shortlived. The affirmation by the council of Florence that there is no contradiction between *a Patre per
Filium* and *ab utroque* has been generally accepted in Latin theology
but has seldom convinced the Greeks.[16] On the eve of the twenty-
first century the divergence regarding the procession of the Holy Spirit
between Orthodoxy and Catholicism has not moved substantially
from where it lay in the eighth and ninth centuries between the Greeks
and the Franks.

This is precisely where something remains to be learned and taken
to heart. In regard to icons and their cult the position is not now
what it was in the *Libri Carolini*. Byzantine and Russian icons are
well known and generally deeply appreciated in Western Christian-
ity. Indeed they are often studied only for their esthetic value and
their technique. They hang in museums and are lavishly reproduced
in books precisely for artistic reasons. But they also have come to
play a spiritual role in Catholic piety that goes far beyond the restrictive position of Gregory I and of the theologians of the Carolingian
monarchy. Most Catholic and Anglican theologians and not a few
Protestants today fully understand and approve the Byzantine devotion to icons, even if this type of devotion takes little room in their
own life and piety. Such a reevaluation is admittedly not identical
with the theological and spiritual function of icons in Orthodoxy.
Yet it represents a remarkable improvement on the antagonistic positions of the ninth century.

There may be another lesson to be learned, not so much from the
controversy itself as from the main lines of Gottschalk's theology. His
descriptions of divine attributes are cumulative. Rather than mention one attribute of God Gottschalk likes to weave a long string of
them. Instead of citing one act or action of God he lists a series. In
his perspective an attribute of God is never thought of by itself, but
always in permanent symbiosis with all others. God's justice presupposes and shares all aspects of divine being, oneness, eternity, truth,
goodness, beauty, immensity, love, mercy, knowledge, foresight, power,
and so on. And God's immensity presupposes and shares all aspects
of divine power, foresight, knowledge, mercy, love, justice, beauty,
goodness, truth, eternity, oneness, being, and so forth. This opens an
extremely dynamic contemplation of the divine actions in creation.

Effected by divine wisdom and power, creation is also filled with all the attributes of God. By the same token this perspective opens to view a principle that should dissolve the dilemma of divine predestination and human free choice, on the horns of which Hincmar was hopeless impaled. This may be called the principle of mutual inclusion: Human creatures are not prisoners of predestination even as Gottschalk, following Augustine, described it, for their creation presupposes and shares all aspects of all the attributes of God, and notably the divine goodness and the empowerment of creaturely freedom. Had Hincmar perceived this the predestinarian controversy could have been avoided and, along with it, the later recurrences of the problem. But neither did Hincmar have this sort of insight nor could Gottschalk fully unfold his thought and belief neatly and clearly.

Ecumenical Perspective

Several popes of the twentieth century, notably Paul VI and John Paul II, have expressed their eagerness to renew the links of ecclesial communion with Orthodoxy. Mutual visits have been made. Fraternal letters have been exchanged. Ecumenical commissions have been created. Orthodox and Catholics are often in agreement in regard to the initiatives of the World Council of Churches and the documents published by its Faith and Order Commission. The hope of reunion for the year 2000 has even been expressed by John Paul II. In spite of new irritants between Orthodox and Catholics that have emerged from the breakup of the USSR, this hope persists, even if it does not seem to be quite realistic.

The chief lesson of the story is clear. The *Filioque* united Hincmar and Gottschalk when they bitterly disagreed in trinitarian theology and each one regarded the other as a heretic. Even when, in the sixteenth century, the Reformers denigrated the scolastic speculation that leads to a "theology of glory" they never questioned the doctrine of the *Filioque* that was part of their heritage from Augustine. Widely diverging on so many other points, the Reformation and the Counterreformation were at one in accepting the doctrine of the double procession of the Spirit and the creed of Nicaea-Constantinople in its interpolated form. One may then wonder if the profession of the *Filioque* has not functioned as a cementing agent that has kept Western Christians together in spite of the breakdown of their ecclesial communion. In the language of George Lindbeck, the *Filioque* has persisted in the West, not perhaps because it encapsulates a "propositional-cognitive" truth,[17] or because it belongs to a necessary "experiential-expressive" structure of faith, but because it has played a positive role as a "cultural-linguistic" agent of unity. But the unity of two that is obtained against a third is never that of full communion.

In regard to the *Filioque* little has been done in modern ecumenical dialogues, and nothing yet has been undone of the mistakes of the past. Uncanonical though its introduction into the Latin creed certainly was, the *Filioque* is still generally used in the Latin Catholic Church and has even been inserted in several of the liturgies of Oriental Churches in communion with the bishop of Rome. It has been translated into all the languages in which the Catholic liturgy is now celebrated. Even though the *Filioque* has been declared optional in some churches that are members of the World Council of Churches, there has been little effort in the West, Catholic or Protestant, to initiate a thorough review of the doctrine. But there can be no restoration of communion with Orthodoxy without at least such an attempt[18]. At stake of course is the authority of Augustine. But Catholic theology departed long ago from the Augustinian view of predestination and of salvation outside the visible limits of the church.[19] It is not bound by what is obsolete or erroneous in Augustine's speculations. And one can well argue that the endorsement of the *Filioque* by some of the general councils of the West was not tantamount to a formal definition of faith.

It would be another mistake, however, to examine again the doctrine of the Trinity as though it were a mere matter of speculation. The Trinity is not first of all a doctrine. It is the halting expression by Christians of what they have perceived in faith of the life of God. Before being food for the mind as doctrine it is first of all food for the heart and soul as experience. It was precisely because both Archbishop Hincmar and the monk Gottschalk perceived the Trinity at that level that they became so concerned about the orthodoxy of the phrase, *trina deitas*. Unfortunately their conflict was not only about the truth of an experience. They fell into the common error of letting their reciprocal distrust, their antagonism over predestination, their resentment of each other's behavior and language, their self-image, and possibly their ambition, interfere with a serene examination of tradition and doctrine. Each made himself unable to listen except to find fault in what the other was saying. True dialogue, we have been reminded by Vatican Council II, requires that the discussants approach each other *par cum pari*,[20] "on an equal basis," so that the other's position is considered at least as a hypothetical possibility for the Christian faith.

The evolution of languages has rendered obsolete the exact point of the trinitarian controversy of the ninth century. Neither English nor the other modern European tongues have a numeral adjective that covers the richness and the ambiguity of the Latin word *trinus*. This has effectively pushed the question between Hincmar and Gottschalk into the penumbra of unresolved theological problems. Yet when they flared at each other about the designation of deity and all divine attributes as "one and trine," they showed us how not to handle the questions that remain between the churches of East and West concerning the one God who is Father, Word, and Spirit.[21]

Notes

[1] Beginning with *Sacris solemniis/ Juncta sint gaudia*, the hymn ends with the following stanza, *Te trina deitas/ Unaque poscimus: / Sic nos tu visita/ Sicut te colimus./ Per tuas semitas/ Duc nos quo tendimus,/ Ad lucem quam inhabitas* (Aquinas Byrnes, ed., *The Hymns of the Dominican Missal and Breviary*, London: Herder Book Company, 1943, p. 174). The hymn was used in the Tridentine liturgy for matins of the feast of Corpus Christi, and was also usually sung in the procession of the day. Each two lines were often printed as one: *Te trina deitas unaque poscimus...* (as in Connelly, *Hymns*, p.122). The hymn was not altered in the liturgical revision of Urban VIII.

[2] The date is given by Claudius's adversary, Dungal the Recluse's *Liber adversus Claudium Turinensem* (PL 105, 481C). The episode in question is narrated by Claudius of Turin in *Apologeticum atque restrictum adversus Theutmirum abbatem* (PL 105, 460D). It is also in Jonas of Orléans's critique of Claudius (PL 106, 310C-311A). Claudius of Turin defended his position in *Liber de imaginibus sanctorum* (PL 104,199-228, where it is erroneously placed among the works of Agobard of Lyon).

[3] One can distinguish between Carolingian art as such, in the confines of the empire of the Franks, Iberian art, and Celtic art in Ireland and in Irish foundations on the continent, though there are close ties between all of them.

[4] Hincmar of Reims had helped raise his nephew when the boy, born around 835-838, lost his mother, the archbishop's sister. Maternal uncle and nephew were closely tied in the mentality of the times, which preserved traces of former matriarchal patterns in Germanic society. The older Hincmar trusted his nephew well enough to choose him for the see of his deceased friend, Pardulus, in 858, when the young man was barely twenty years of age. One may surmise that the younger Hincmar had seen his uncle defend the prerogatives of the see of Reims. As an adult he defended the rights and possessions of the see of Laon against both archbishop and king.

[5] McKeon, *Hinkmar*, p.268, note 54.

[6] John VIII had fled from Italy when Lambert, duke of Spoleto, invaded the papal territories; he once again sought help from the Franks.

[7] Mansi, XI, 960.

[8] Peter Brown, *The Book of Kells*, London: Thames and Hudson, 1980.

[9] See my studies of religious poetry: *Poetry and Contemplation in St John of the Cross*, Athens, OH: Ohio University Press, 1988; *Juana Inés de la Cruz and the Theology of Beauty. The First Mexican Theology*, Notre Dame, IN: University of Notre Dame Press, 1991. On the way symbols function, see *La Théologie parmi les sciences humaines*, p.75-93.

[10] PL 125, 823BC.

[11] See DS 805. This endorsement, however, was done in passing and does not qualify as a formal definition of faith.

[12] See DS 806: "Between the Creator and the creature one cannot notice a similarity without having to notice a greater dissimilarity."

[13] Tavard, *Vision*, p.74-78.

[14] *Decree pro Jacobitis*, DS 1330.

[15] DS 853.

[16] *Decree pro Graecis*, DS 1300-1302. The various decrees addressed by the council of Florence to oriental Christians who wished to renew their communion with Rome ought to be read as high level catechetical instructions rather than formal definitions. The union effected at Florence in 1439 was repudiated in Constantinople in 1450 under Patriarch Gregorios III Mammas. Mark Eugenikos, bishop of Ephesus (died, 1444), was the chief opponent of the

compromise of Florence. Its main defensor, Hieromonk Bessarion (1395-1472), settled in Rome and became a cardinal in 1439; he refused to be elected to the papacy in 1471.

[17] George Lindbeck, *The Nature of Doctrine. Religion and Theology in a post-Liberal Age*, Philadelphia: Westminster Press, 1984. Lindbeck does not himself apply his categories to the *Filioque*.

[18] A Clarification issued by the Pontifical Council for the Unity of Christians (13 Septemebr 1995) offers an elaborate survey of the question. Briefly, the Eastern and Western traditions are not contradictory, if it is admitted that the Latin *processio* has another meaning then the Greek ἐχπόρευσις. Thus one may say, "the Spirit originates from the Father alone and proceeds from the Father and the Son." This is seen as the intended sense of the condensed formulation of the councils of Lyon II and Florence: "the Spirit proceeds from the Father through the Son." See the full text in *Information Service* (The Pontifical Council for Promoting Christian Unity, N. 89 (1995/II-III), p. 88-92.

[19] Francis A. Sullivan, *Salvation outside the Church? Tracing the History of the Catholic Response*, New York: Paulist Press, 1992.

[20] *Unitatis redintegratio*, n.9.

[21] The *Catechism of the Catholic Church* presents the Unity and Trinity of God in a contrasted perspective: "La Trinité est Une... L'Unité divine est Trine." (I evidently cite the French edition, *Catéchisme de l'Eglise catholique*, Paris: Mame/Plon, 1992, n. 253-54, p. 63). The text is presumably quoting Pope Pelagius, though without acknowledgement or further explanation. But these expressions are identically those of Gottschalk; the second was rejected by Hincmar as heretical and defended by Gottschalk as orthodox. I doubt that the authors intended to review the controversy of the ninth century. It is one of the ironies of the Catholic tradition that what raised theological tempers at one time can pass unnoticed in another period. The official English translation ("The Trinity is One.... The divine Unity is Tri-une," in the *Catechism of the Catholic Church*, New York: Doubleday, 1995, n. 253-54, p. 75) misses the contrast, *One/Trine*, since *one* is included in *tri-une*. By the same token the sentence says nothing about unity. This translation of course eliminates any possible connection with Pope Pelagius and with Gottschalk's trinitarian theology. Incidentally,

the word, trine, is included in *Webster's New World Dictionary of the English language*, as well as in the *Compact Edition of the Oxford Dictionary of the English Language*, 1971.

EPILOGUE

Hincmar gave Gottschalk a telling and savage epitaph when he wrote of the monk's death: *abiit in locum suum*. The locus in question could be no other than the hell of unrepentant heretics. The monk did not compose an epitaph for the archbishop, but since he considered his tormentor a vicious heretic he might have penned something similar in return.

Hincmar, however, wrote an epitaph for himself:

Nomine non merito praesul Hincmarus ab antro
Te, lector tituli, quaeso: memento mei,
Quem grege pastorum proprio Dionysius olim
Remorum populis, ut petiere, dedit,
Quique humilis magnae Remensis regmina plebis
Rexi pro modulo, hic modo verme voror.
Ergo animae requiem nunc et, cum carne resumpta,
Gaudia plena mihi, haec quoque posce simul:
Christe, tui clemens famuli miserere fidelis.
Sis pia cultori, sancta Maria, tuo.
Dulcis Remigii sibimet devotio prosit,
Qua te dilexit pectore et ore, manu.
Quare hic suppetiit lex sua membra locari;
Ut bene complacuit, denique sic obiit.[1]

Lord by name, not by merit, I, Hincmar, from the tomb
Beg you who read this inscription: Remember me.
Formerly Denys gave me as shepherd to his flock,
The people of Reims, as they asked.
Humbly I governed this great people
As best I could. Here I am now worm-eaten.
Both for the peace of my soul, and at the resurrection
For my full joys, I ask you for these prayers:
"Christ, in clemency have mercy on your faithful servant!
"Be kind, Holy Mary, to your devotee!
"May his sweet piety toward Remi be good to him
"By which he loved you with heart, lips, and hands.

"For here the law made his remains to be laid;
"As it pleased him well, then he so died."

The archbishop died at Epernay as he was fleeing a Viking raid. The MGH edition specifies that it was on the fourth day of the seventh month of the thirty-seventh year of his episcopate, which was also the eight hundred and eighty-second year of the incarnation of the Lord. A footnote adds that this was the twelfth day of the calends of January, 882.[2] Hincmar was buried in the cathedral of Reims near the monument he had built for the earthly remains of St Remi, his great predecessor.

Gottschalk did not write his own epitaph. Yet from the three poems he addressed to Christ the Savior he could have chosen many a stanza for a funeral inscription, as for instance,

Esto salvator   simul et ducator,
sis gubernator   velut es creator,
sis triumphator   mihi sive victor
          et superator.
          Amen.[3]

Be Savior   and my Leader
Be Providence   as you are Creator
Be to me Conqueror   or Winner
          And Dominator.
          Amen.

Largely ignored in their native lands, that are now parts of France or Germany, Hincmar and Gottschalk have only been given a few lines and an occasional footnote in histories of Christian doctrines, and they have intrigued a few devoted scholars. One may indeed learn something, as I have tried to show, from their tragic clashes. Yet one may also hold them reconciled, in spite of themselves, in the church's memory.

Notes
[1] PL 125, 17-18; MGH, *Poetae*, II, p. 420.
[2] Migne gives the date of death as 21 December 881.
[3] *Orationes metricae* III, stanza 12 (MHG, *Poetae*, III, p.728).

INDEX